CASEY WEADE

JOB OPTIONAL*

*The **science** of retiring with **confidence**;
the **art** of living with **purpose**.

Casey Weade/Howard Bailey Financial™
6526 West Jefferson Blvd.
Fort Wayne, IN 46804
www.HowardBailey.com

Job Optional*/ Casey Weade—1st ed.
ISBN 978-1944194543

I would like to dedicate this book to my wife and rock, Chelsie, and my two boys, Calvin and Carver, who are my greatest purpose in life.

PRAISE FOR JOB OPTIONAL*

"In his new book, Casey has brought his experience and stories to really drive home what retirement is all about, and how to achieve it successfully. This is great food for thought for those approaching retirement."

~Dr. Wade Pfau, Professor of Retirement Income at The American College,
Author & Founder of Retirement Researcher

"Casey delivers a very personal and powerful message in his book Job Optional and continues to move the needle forward for the financial planning profession. This is a must read for anyone doing retirement income planning."

~Jamie Hopkins, J.D., LL.M., CFP,
Director of Retirement Research at Carson Group

"Casey Weade delivers sound wisdom packaged in a fresh, relevant form. Dive into his content and you'll grow yourself as well as your assets."

~Kary Oberbrunner, Speaker, Coach, Author of *Day Job to Dream Job*

"A unique and refreshing take on breaking free from your 9 to 5 and preparing for your dream retirement; not just the financial side, but the emotions that come along with beginning a new chapter and making sure your Golden Years are fulfilling."

~Dr. Hans Finzel, best-selling author of *Launch Your Encore*,
President of HDLeaders

"A must read for sound financial guidance. Casey compacts 10+ years' worth of retirement planning experience into an easy-to-follow guide to having the financial freedom to step away from your job and into your next chapter."

~Cody Foster, Co-Founder & Owner of Advisor's Excel

"Most investment professionals focus strictly on the financial side of retirement planning. But Casey Weade believes retirement planning should start with the question, "What does a purposeful retirement mean to you?" His book will help you create a meaningful retirement that is both financially secure and personally rewarding. Using his advice, the rest of your life really can be the best of your life."

~Nancy Collamer, author of *Second-Act Careers: 50+ Ways to Profit from Your Passions During Retirement*

TABLE OF CONTENTS

CHAPTER ONE:
BASIC LESSONS LEARNED FROM THE GREATEST GENERATION

CHAPTER TWO:
PURPOSE-BASED ASSET ALLOCATION

CHAPTER THREE:
LIQUIDITY PLANNING

CHAPTER FOUR:
INCOME PLANNING

CHAPTER FIVE:
GROWTH PLANNING

CHAPTER SIX:
ESTATE PLANNING

CHAPTER SEVEN:
CLOSING

A NOTE FROM THE AUTHOR

I have had the opportunity to work with some amazing clients over the years and have developed wonderful and long-term relationships with many of them. Not only do I appreciate the opportunity to work with them, but I value the trust I have developed with them.

The people whose financial lives are discussed in this book are a composite of many clients I have worked with over the years. As you might expect, the names, situations, and personal details shared throughout the book have been changed to protect their privacy.

INTRODUCTION

NOT YOUR TYPICAL MONEY BOOK

This isn't your typical financial book looking to sell you on a product or service; it's unfiltered and frank advice offering actionable items to implement in your personal and financial life. This book is a guide to help you pursue the retirement you have always dreamed of.

This book is about discovering and deciding what your life's purpose is and how to live it to the fullest in "retirement."

For you, retirement may mean that you stop working and enjoy each day without the worry of how you will pay for everything.

Or perhaps for you, retirement means the freedom to quit your current job at a moment's notice with financial confidence and live out your passions.

Or maybe you never want to stop working, and for you, retiring simply means being able to fund your professional passions without sacrificing your personal endeavors.

Whatever retirement means to you, if you're ready to take the planning of it seriously, you've found the right place to start. We are about to take a deep dive into retirement planning, covering a broad range of topics, risks, ideas and strategies—no holds barred. To have a truly confident retirement, you might have to do some legwork and dig deep.

There is no silver bullet for your retirement years, despite what you may have been told. There are no perfect investments, or plans, for that matter, but if you can identify the specific purpose for your life savings, you can find the most efficient way of getting there.

Once you have a solid understanding of the risks you will face and an outline of the specific strategies to overcome each risk, you can start enjoying the money you saved and stop thinking about it not being there when you need it most.

BASIC LESSONS LEARNED FROM THE GREATEST GENERATION

I remember it like it was yesterday. I was 8 years old, sitting in my grandparents' living room in the small town of Ligonier, Indiana, on a Saturday afternoon. My grandparents lived in a modest home on Second Street, just a few blocks from the city park where my dad played as a child. Usually when I remember the times I spent at my grandparents' home, I remember them sitting around the dining room table playing cards or reading the paper. This Saturday was no different. My grandfather, Howard, was reading the newspaper and my grandmother, Christine, was playing Solitaire with actual playing cards (at the time, I didn't even know it was possible to play that game without a computer). I sat in the living room playing with my favorite toy, an old wooden train set that was handed down from a prior generation. I had trouble putting this train set down for anything, much like my own son—by the scale of the tantrum he throws, you'd think it was the end of the world when it's time to put down old Thomas the Train. But this afternoon, something was different. I heard a noise we don't too often hear anymore—one that excites most children (and, I think, anyone with an inner child).

What could it be, this tinkling noise I heard as it passed through the neighborhood of Second Street? You may have already guessed; it was the ice cream man, bearing a truck loaded with any number of frozen treats to delight neighborhood children. As soon as I heard the noise, I jumped out of my seat, knocking my favorite train right off the tracks, and ran to the back of the house. Everyone has a favorite item from the ice cream man, and mine was a red, white and blue BOMB POP. I knew exactly what I wanted, there was only one problem. Like many 8-year-olds, I was a bit short on money.

But I knew where to get some.

I burst past my grandparents, where they serenely sat in the dining room, as I rushed to the back of the house and dove to the closet in my grandparents' bedroom. On my knees, I thrust boots and old books out of the way until BINGO! I'd found it, my grandfather's precious coin collection. My grandfather was an avid coin collector. He had old steel pennies, silver dollars, buffalo nickels, all kinds of good stuff that, to my young mind, wasn't getting any good use just sitting in the back of a musty closet. I grabbed one of his old tattered coin books, knocked out a handful of precious BOMB POP-buying coins, and ran to the front door as fast as I could. I had been too slow to catch the ice cream man before, and that was not going to happen today!

Before I could even grasp the handle to scoot over the threshold, my grandfather had his hand on my arm and alarm in his eyes. I missed the ice cream man that day, as well as the red, white and blue BOMB POP that I had lusted after. Yet, what I did get from that day was something much more valuable.

That sunny day was my first real lesson about money—one that would stick with me and shape my life for decades to come.

I've found we all have a memory like this one, an experience that shapes the way we treat our finances, our business or our relationships for the rest of our lives. Psychologists say these memories often come from traumatic experiences as children—usually between 5 and 10. They may come in the form of an alcoholic father, a drug-addicted mother, bankruptcy, homelessness or death. They can, of course, also be positive experiences. In my case, to my child's mind, I thought missing out on my BOMB POP was pretty traumatic, but looking back, it's easily recognizable as an overwhelmingly positive lesson.

Lessons I've Learned

My Lesson:
The Value Of A Dollar

My grandfather shared with me many things I didn't understand in that moment. For one, he addressed my feelings about using 50 cents to buy my favorite popsicle. My thought, of course was, "Why not? It's just sitting there not doing anything at all, and we have the opportunity to turn it into something delicious for immediate enjoyment!" My grandfather very seriously said, "When I was a boy, we didn't have two nickels to rub together, let alone 50 cents to buy a popsicle." My grandfather was a member of "The Greatest Generation," born just a few years before the Great Depression. His parents lost nearly everything, and his earliest memories were formed watching them struggle to put food on the table. This created a great deal of skepticism and conservativism in my grandfather.

My Grandfather's Lesson:
Savings Over Investment

I also learned the Great Depression was responsible for another "quirk" I couldn't understand about my grandparents, something they would often eat called "coffee soup." I've found many different names for this meal, if you want to call it that, over the years. It was a piece of Sunbeam White Bread—none of this suburban whole grain stuff—topped with brown sugar and drowned in a cup of coffee. I couldn't understand why anyone would subject themselves to such torture, but both my grandparents ate it fairly regularly. Why? Because it was born out of the experiences they had when they were between the ages of five and ten, setting patterns that in many ways were the blueprint for how they would treat their finances for the rest of their lives.

My grandfather was a carpet layer by trade and my grandmother worked in a local factory. They didn't make a lot of money, but what they made they saved. They saved it in the local federal credit union where they knew it was safe. Unfortunately, there was a major embezzlement at this banking institution before credit unions carried NCUA coverage, much like the FDIC insurance you are probably more familiar with. When the scandal broke, my dad was at that impressionable age between 5 and 10. Watching his parents during the ensuing financial hardships of rebuilding the lost savings led him to lean in on that financially conservative nature, as well.

These stories, imparted in lieu of a much-coveted BOMB POP, shaped my way of thinking about saving, spending, and investing as a child, but what happened later created the foundation from which I teach finance today. In 2005, my grandfather passed away at age 78. At the time, I was studying finance in college, learning about the miracles of the stock market and investing in ways my grandfather would never have considered flirting with. When he passed away, it was hard on my family, but the emotional toll was greatest on my grandmother, who was left to pick up the pieces.

My Grandmother's Lesson: Never Lose Money

You see, though my grandmother had the support of my father, who was a financial advisor at the time, as well as my plucky young self, my grandfather did not make his passing easy on her due to his conservative and rather stubborn nature. He did very little in the way of estate planning to help ensure a smooth transition, and, perhaps more vexing, we had our work cut out for us in determining just where their money was in the first place. Sure, there were bank accounts, fixed annuities, certificates of deposit, etc., but there was also a significant amount of money hidden within the house they lived in on Second Street itself. Every visit became an opportunity to find more cash, not just the coin collection my grandfather left behind, but cold hard cash.

One day, I was cleaning through the small hallway pantry when I discovered an old Maxwell Coffee House can that had obviously been there forever, covered in rust. I reached back, opened the can and found several thousand dollars in rolled up bills. You see, my grandparents didn't invest like we are told we must invest today to be successful. Raised in the aftermath of a massive stock market crash, they would never imagine owning a stock, bond or mutual fund.[1] With the experiences my grandfather had with the stock market and the FCU later down the road, he would never risk losing a dime of his hard-earned money.

Make no mistake, it was *hard*-earned. I often hear people complain they don't make enough money to ever retire— either their company doesn't offer a pension, or their Social Security benefits just won't be enough. My grandparents never saw a six-figure income, never made a 10 percent return on their investments; they just worked hard and saved. Most importantly, they followed Warren Buffett's No. 1 Rule of Investing: "Never Lose Money," and never overlooked rule No. 2: "Never Forget Rule No. 1." They also followed Dave Ramsey's common-sense approach to finance (build an emergency fund, get out of debt and stay there, etc.) before Dave was even a twinkle in his mother's eye. They retired in their 60s and enjoyed a wonderful retirement on a pittance of a pension and little-to-no Social Security income.

When my grandmother passed away in 2013, it was the most painful loss of a loved one I had ever endured. I was incredibly close to her; she taught me not just about responsibility, but most importantly she showed me how to enjoy life to the fullest, not to take it too seriously, and to always remember to laugh, no matter the situation. When she passed away, I may have learned an even more important lesson I hope to pass on to anyone reading. Believe it or not, this penny-pinching retired factory worker left behind over a million dollars to my dad and his sister. My mind was blown. Everything I learned in college and all I was taught while completing my boards in pursuit of becoming a CERTIFIED FINANCIAL PLANNER™ practitioner went out the window.

The Great Recession Lesson: Be Cautious and Conservative

In my opinion, over the last few decades, we have slowly lost touch with this way of treating our finances. We have been brainwashed by the mammoth financial industry today into thinking that we need to take on significant risks both in the way of investing and approaching debt to be successful. This mindset, I might add, was proliferated in the '80s and '90s, when most of today's financial advisors got their start in this business.

Prior to 1974, we didn't have things like 401(k)s. Instead, many relied on the pension plans of the companies they worked for to provide their future retirement, with a golden watch to boot. In 1974, the Employee Retirement Income Security Act was passed, also known as ERISA, introducing 401(k)s to the masses. Now, the largest generation in history could take money out of their paycheck and invest it directly in the stock market.

On top of this, the advent of the internet led to the first internet brokerage firm in August 1994, K. Aufhauser & Company, Inc., later acquired by TD Ameritrade. Brokerage firms popped up on every street corner and shopping mall to help us get a piece of the biggest bull market in history. If you think about it, stock market investing for the masses has only been around for a short period of time. Throughout the early 2000s, investors were smacked with reality twice as the market lost half of its value. It was during this period that I began practicing in the investing and financial world as part of what will be known as "the Great Recession generation," yet continuing the cautious and conservative nature of previous generations in my family.

My Dad's Lesson: Don't Get Overconfident, Stocks Aren't for Everyone

My dad wasn't without financial turmoil in his own life, which lent itself to many learning opportunities for me, in addition to the lessons I learned from my grandparents. Much of my parents' wealth was made in their real estate investing escapades. In an unfortunate series of events, we watched as most of it crumbled during the 2008 financial crisis and real estate bubble.

It wasn't always that way, of course. As a kid, I remember living in a small apartment, but by the mid- '90s, Dad had purchased his own apartment complex, made up of 40 units. This became like a family farm to us: My dad and grandfather laid carpet on the weekends, my mother balanced the books and cleaned after renters moved out, my other grandfather (Ralph) helped get new renters their keys, and I often spent weekends keeping the grounds clean and picking up the trash that seemed to have so much trouble hitting the dumpsters. If you've ever owned rentals, then you know the property management side of the business is not for the lazy. My dad took a loan out for the purchase of the property, later paying it off with the sale of the property just after the tech crash of the 2000s.

In the '80s, my father started a second career as a financial advisor. I remember asking my mom if Dad could come outside and play, but he was busy studying for his securities license at the time. Like many people, he wholeheartedly bought into the booming stock market and the opportunities it offered. Not only did he place his IRAs and his non-real estate investments in mutual funds but would often pressure my grandfather to do the same. I remember sitting around the dining room table eating supper at my grandparents' while my dad would pull out his personal investment statements, brag about his returns, and flaunt them to my grandfather, trying to show him what his money should be doing. Meanwhile, my grandfather would grumble, stuck in his ways, saying, "It'll all come crashing down, you'll see!" Well, he was right; the tech bubble peaked on March 10, 2000.

Shortly after, we saw the terrorist attacks of Sept. 11, 2001, drag the market down even further. My father lost more than half his life's savings in three short years. I can remember him sitting in his home office every day, logged into his brokerage account just trying to get back to even. You see, while the stock market may have *only* been down around 40 percent, many investors lost substantially more due to the over-weighted tech sector in many mutual funds. It took him years to make up his losses…he recovered right in time for the financial crisis of 2008.

Luckily, by that time Dad had decided the stock market wasn't for him. When he experienced the losses of 2000-2003 firsthand, he had just sold his apartment complex. He couldn't imagine enduring the kind of losses that he had experienced in his other investments without the cash from the sale of what was probably the best investment he ever made. Not only was it one of the best investments he had ever made, but he saw it as a family investment. Blood, sweat and tears of multiple generations went into those apartments and Dad wouldn't be able to stand losing a dime.

On a related note, I find this to be very true for self-created wealth—whether it is an entrepreneurial business, farm or other real estate investment, most of these individuals who have worked to build something don't want to risk not only their life's savings, but the blood, sweat and tears of multiple generations. Contrast this to the average 401(k) investor who built most of their wealth by piling money into the mutual funds in their employer's retirement plan. The latter individuals are often more comfortable with the extreme volatility seen in the public markets.

Why is this an important point? When I meet with entrepreneurs (farmers, real estate moguls, business owners, etc.), I find they can typically relate to not wanting to risk their life savings. By having a stronger connection to their money, they usually make smarter, more conservative decisions that lead to longer term success as opposed to those who just watched their 401(k)s ebb and flow.

From those days forward, Dad put his money almost exclusively in fixed income and real estate investments; he was never going back to a market that could wash away half of his wealth overnight. This mentality of protection and conservativism would continue into another generation.

The Common Cents Of Generations Past

In large part, I feel we have lost touch with the commonsense and conservative approach of past generations. Instead, we've been trained to seek get-rich-quick schemes, big returns, the next best investment or the silver bullet that will make us wealthy overnight. I'm here to tell you these things don't exist. There are those who have hit the home run in the lottery or with lucky investments, but they could have just as easily struck out.

Striking out in retirement isn't where you want to end up. Whether you have taken market risks with your 401(k) to accumulate your wealth, owned a business that could have ended at any time due to the unknown, taken on debt to finance real estate that could have defaulted—no matter *how* you made it, you've made it. You've made it to the glory land called retirement. It's time to preserve your wealth and make it last a lifetime. It's time to look back on the Greatest Generation and take a page from their book. This all starts with deciding what you want out of retirement in the first place.

The Definition Of Retirement

You may be wondering, when are we going to get to the financial advice and investment recommendations? The reality is, while most financial advisors start there, it should really be where you finish. I've seen far too many retirees quit working only to be lost in the day-to-day monotony of retirement. I learned this firsthand, as I watched my father try and fail at his own retirement by doing just that.

Is Playing Golf Enough?

My dad retired early by anybody's standards at the ripe age of 50 after selling a successful insurance brokerage firm with several hundred agents across the country and flipping dozens of real estate properties along the way. He had always been a hardworking nose-to-the-grindstone kind of guy with big goals. Unfortunately, most of those goals were monetary, lacking the real substance needed to find happiness in retirement. He had accumulated enough assets and decided he didn't need to work anymore, so that's exactly what he did. Retiring to the lake and the golf course, he thought he had it all figured out. My dad and I were both avid golfers, playing almost every single day and any opportunity that presented itself.

Dad would usually get to the golf course just before dawn broke, and since I was a bag boy working at the golf course where he was a member, I would have to be there even earlier to get the carts prepped, coffee made and bags loaded. He got his handicap down to zero, a scratch golfer, meaning he would on average shoot par—for those unfamiliar with golf, it means on an average day he was a first-class player. Then, something awful happened.

He got what we call "the yips." If you're not familiar with "the yips," it's the worst thing that can happen to a golfer. In a matter of days, a lights-out putter went from knocking in five-footers without a practice stroke to being unable to make a six-inch putt. It was truly sad to watch, and so we usually didn't. When it was Dad's turn to putt, everyone in his group would typically close their eyes or turn their backs. You see, while the yips are one hundred percent psychological, they are oddly contagious. I wasn't immune myself, struggling with my putting for years after watching my dad's golf game completely fall apart. Golf was what he had built his retirement on, and now it was gone. It became one of the most depressing areas of his life, so he gave it up.

To Work Or Not To Work?

Without a higher purpose or calling in his life, Dad floundered. Without golf—or something better to do—he quickly decided he was happier working. He launched a new career as a financial advisor after just a couple of short years of retirement.

As I write this book, Dad is beginning to prepare for his second attempt at retirement. He has found a passion for travel and helping others enjoy their travel to the fullest. Not only that, but he has a couple of grandkids to help him make up for any lost time we missed when I was a kid. Forty hours was a part-time job when I was little and, as a result, I spent most of my time between my mother and grandparents. Now, Dad has a second chance at retirement and has found a purpose for all his free time—it will be time well spent with family and pursuing his new passions.

My father is in the perfect place I call Job Optional. He can now choose to work or not work; to keep building his career contributions, fulfill personal passions, or both. He is in control. He is an example of the science behind retiring and the art of retiring with purpose.

> TRUTH: IT'S NOT THE SIZE OF YOUR BANK ACCOUNT. FROM THOUSANDAIRES TO BILLIONAIRES, PEOPLE FIND TRUE HAPPINESS BY FINDING AND FULFILLING THEIR PURPOSE IN LIFE.

What Is A Purpose-Based Retirement (PBR)?

After working one-on-one with thousands of people planning for retirement, I can tell you without hesitation that this planning must start with a purpose. Successful retirement planning is all about a purposeful life.

So, what do I mean when I say, "purposeful life?" Here are a few real-life examples of people who retired with purpose and how it impacted them.

Retired with Purpose: Patrick and Brenda
Their Purpose: "Creating the marriage we never could."

One of the happiest couples I have ever worked with, leading one of the most fulfilling retirements I have ever seen, aren't the wealthiest in savings, but are by far the wealthiest in life. Patrick and Brenda were working as an engineer and a nurse, looked forward to retiring with a few hundred thousand dollars and a pension and were not the happiest people when we first met. During our initial visit, they never broke a smile.

They often discussed their pessimistic outlook on the economy and focused on how politics could put their future and that of their children in jeopardy. Up until then, their careers consisted of working competing hours, raising four children and missing out on what they described as "a lifetime with one another." They had never seen the Grand Tetons, Glacier National Park, or even Nashville, for that matter.

While they were true pessimists, they were crystal-clear about what they wanted for their retirement. Their purpose in finalizing a retirement strategy was to simply start over by building the life they always wanted but never had.

After we had finalized their retirement plans, the first thing they did was renew their vows and set out on the honeymoon they had never taken. They ultimately purchased an RV, got a new dog, and began traveling the country, essentially starting over with the purpose of creating—in their words—"the marriage we could never have."

They now attend all our private client events and quarterly reviews with the biggest smiles of any clients I have ever worked with, often saying they are happier than they have ever been.

Prior to implementing their very own Purpose-Based Retirement strategy, they worried about all the unknown risks they faced in retirement and how it could all be over in a blink of an eye. Once we laid out the major risks they would face in retirement and, more importantly, structured a plan to address each one systematically, they said those worries went away. By having a plan for the worst-case scenario, they could turn off the news channels and move on with life—on their own terms.

Now, everyone is different. For you, waiting until retirement to really begin living your dream life may be your preference. Or maybe for you, retiring is just a second act.

Retired with Purpose: My Mentor
His Purpose: "To be and create."

Years ago, I was introduced to a business owner who had started his business in the family barn, growing it to a $100 million company.

Being part of the advisory team for the sale of the company was one of the most fulfilling and exciting experiences I have ever had as an advisor. Seeing someone start something from scratch, change hundreds of lives and influence global retail in the process was inspiring. We spent dozens of hours together prior to the sale of the business, discussing purpose and what the next stage of life would look like. Along the way he helped me discover my purpose in life and in business, becoming one of my closest friends and mentors. After the sale of the business, he decided to pursue starting a new business from the ground up that he felt had the potential to change the world. He had never had the time or resources to devote to his new endeavor until he "retired." Now, he spends most of his time building an even more influential company, fulfilling his purpose, which he stated as "to be and create." He could do this because he had a Purpose-Based Retirement to fall back on, allowing him to focus on his true purpose for this next stage of his life and put the worries of "money" behind him. His story is unique in terms of the scale of his projects, but I have seen many retirees with this same mentality.

Typically, they are highly driven entrepreneurs and thinkers; these individuals almost shouldn't retire, as it would be a shock to their system. For many of these gifted men and women, "retiring" from creating, inventing and using their God-given gifts to change the world for the better would truly be a loss to society. Not everyone has these talents, but if you do, don't squander them or you will eventually look back with regret!

For these movers and shakers, this is not a reason to ignore retirement planning—the financial realities of retirement are ultimately impossible to avoid. On the contrary, if you have a retirement plan to fall back on, then you can take bigger risks in following the new dreams you long to fulfill—dreams you may not have been able to pursue during your working career. This may not be as big as starting a whole new career. It may be as simple as part-time work or contract work in the previous career you are familiar with because you still have so much to offer.

Retired with Purpose: Ralph Bailey

His Purpose: "Helping students, teachers and educational leaders throughout the state."

My maternal grandfather, Ralph Bailey, was one of those individuals. My grandfather became the school principal of Etna-Troy, a school for grades one through eight, at the age of 25. He later became a superintendent of schools. He eventually became one of the most influential people in the education system in Indiana, helping to shape the political world of education for years to come. The state recognized him with the Sagamore of the Wabash, an award for his work in education. At the time, it was the highest honor which the governor of Indiana could bestow as a personal tribute, usually given to those who provided distinguished service to the state or to the governor. When I called to wish my grandfather a happy birthday on his 86th birthday, he told me he was just offered a three-year extension on his contract as superintendent of Smith-Green Community Schools, a local school corporation. In his 90s, my grandfather still began every morning with putting on a suit and then going to work to manage a full schedule helping students, teachers, and educational leaders throughout the state. All the while, he had a retirement plan; he didn't need to work, but he continued fulfilling a higher purpose, which helped to keep him one of the sharpest 90-somethings I have ever met.

Not all retirees choose traveling, starting a new career or consulting to fulfill their purpose. Some are more spiritual quests.

Retired with Purpose: Rick and Jeannette
Their Purpose: "Starting their own church in a small town"

One couple I worked with, Rick and Jeannette, spent their careers traveling the country, climbing the corporate ladder from one Fortune 500 CFO position to the next. They were referred to me by another client of mine, as they were looking to make a transition to a retirement specialist and local advisor before their move back home to Indiana from Texas. Our visits together were almost entirely online, since Rick would work long hours in his job out of state.

Despite the corporate expense account and every trapping of power, Rick was a humble man with humble goals, and our conversations often focused on his and Jeannette's purpose in retirement and what they wanted their money to accomplish for them. Rick often lamented that Jeannette, who had retired, spent her time flying out to spend time with their grandchildren, while he felt trapped at work, stuck doing something he didn't enjoy and offered no challenge.

While the company had presented him with the prospect of making more income than he could ever imagine if he stayed, you could feel Rick's angst, as he knew it just wasn't that important anymore. Staying meant that he was earning money he and Jeannette would never be able to spend while forgoing some of the most meaningful experiences of his life. They had a dream of starting their own church in a small town just outside of Huntington, Indiana. They had saved multi-millions throughout his working career and weren't big spenders. After helping to build and examine their budget, they needed less than $100,000 per year in after-tax income to live the life they were accustomed to. They had nearly $70,000 per year in pension and Social Security benefits even before they factored in the millions of savings. The quick math: they had way more than they needed. This lent itself to a grand discussion regarding risk, as he was one whom many would regard as having more than enough to afford taking on substantial risk with his retirement for greater growth opportunities. However, he said to me, "Casey, why would we take the risk if we don't need to? If we just preserve what we have and don't lose it, we will have enough money to last for the rest of our lives without worries."

There is a great lesson to be learned here, as even though Rick had been trained to take risks his entire working life to be successful, he recognized he had "made it" and he didn't want to worry about it anymore. By structuring a Purpose-Based Retirement focused on preserving their life savings, Rick and Jeannette could focus on the more important things in their life—like spending more time in the church and with family—rather than what stock they should pick next.

Retired with Purpose: The Doctor
His Purpose: "Give away time and expertise to those in need."

Another gentleman I worked with was a physician who felt frustrated with what he saw in a money-driven medical community and set out to give his time and experience away to those in need all over the world. As he finally made his transition into retirement, he often asked why he didn't start sooner. He always felt he didn't have enough money to retire and was making too much to quit. The reality was that he had created enough wealth to last the rest of his life years prior to our first meeting, but he never sat down and really examined his retirement to determine what was possible. As a result, he lost time he will never get back, but now that he has a plan that will allow him to move on to fulfill his purpose, he says he'll never look back. He spends his time giving back to the world and serves on boards to positively impact change in the medical community. Whatever you decide doesn't have to be grandiose, but without thinking, you will look back at some point in your life with regret, wondering what would have been possible if you had just taken the time to plan and reflect.

How To Start Practicing For Retirement

One of the best ways for you to start this journey is to practice your retirement. Envision what you will do and how you will spend your days. This can start with simply planning out what you might want a day in retirement to look like.

What time do you wake up?

Where do you have breakfast?

Who do you spend your time with throughout the day?

What time do you have dinner and where?

What time do you go to bed?

Playing out a full day of retirement is just the start, then you can take the next step to envision your month-to-month and year-to-year plans.

When interviewing Nancy Collamer for the *Retire with Purpose* podcast, author of *Second-Act Careers: 50+ Ways to Profit from Your Passions During Semi-Retirement*, she walked through how she coaches pre-retirees to outline their "ideal" day in retirement and how to create the "ideal" year in retirement. I especially enjoyed the word "ideal," as it's one thing to envision just another day in retirement, but a perfect day helps deepen your perspective. I prefer to walk our clients through first identifying a typical day and then using that foundation to begin making edits to envision what an "ideal" or perfect day would look like.

Identify the gaps in your time and how you will fill them. Going from full speed to a dead stop can cause significant trauma, so prepare yourself for what your life might be. This is the start of creating your very own Purpose-Based Retirement. After you have identified your purpose, then—and only then—can you set out to organize your assets in such a way to most efficiently accomplish that purpose.

Retired with Purpose: YOU?
Your Purpose: What drives you?

Have you thought about what makes you tick? What gets you passionate? What do you want to dedicate your time, energy and money to outside of your career? Have you considered how important working is to you—how you will feel if you no longer work day to day?

One of the challenges I face when working with new clients is identifying the answers to these questions. The reason is because what motivates people is deeply personal and individual.

There was a study conducted in 2000 called the Cornell Retirement and Well-Being Study, which concluded that about 44 percent of retirees worked for pay after their retirement began. Did they need the money? Were they bored? Why take a job after retiring from the workforce? The answers are in what drives you personally.

The study went on to detail that, of those currently employed after retirement, 14 percent say they will "never retire" and 28 percent say they will work "as long as I am healthy." Most want their time to be filled with personal passions and new experiences.

Other reasons for returning to work after retiring:

- Have free time – 73%

- Desire additional income – 63%

- Not ready to retire – 58%

- Maintain social contacts – 56%

15 Motivations To Consider In PBR

When considering your Job Optional status and a Purpose Based Retirement, you have to determine what motivates you. There are dozens of motivating factors. Here are a few of my favorites to consider when thinking about your purpose and how your financial confidence fits into that purpose.

#1   Accomplishments – to collect experiences

#2 – Action – to stay relevant and active

#3 – Authority – to be a leader and contributor

#4 – Belonging – to feel a part of something bigger

#5 – Creativity – to express your artistic side

#6 – Friendship – to stay connected to a social circle

#7 – Identity – to feel like yourself through actions

#8 – Intellectual Stimulation – to keep your brain engaged

#9 – Lifelong Learning – to continue to develop new skills

#10 – Making a Difference – to leave a legacy and impact

#11 – Mentoring – to pass on your knowledge to others

#12 – Passion – to engage in what makes you feel most alive

#13 – Problem-Solving – to contribute to a solution

#14 – Self-Esteem – to feel good through contribution

#15 – Value – to provide value to others and feel valued

Patrick and Michelle designed their PBR around #12 – Passion and #4 – Belonging by committing to a new life that brought them closer together through their shared passions.

My mentor designed his PBR around #3 – Authority, #11 – Mentoring, and #15 – Value by creating a second career not based on needing money but on providing support and education to people who motivated him.

Ralph Bailey designed his PBR around #1 – Accomplishments, #7 – Indentity, and #10 – Making a Difference, working to inspire others until his final days. That was my grandfather's legacy.

Rick and Jeannette designed their PBR around #4 – Belonging and #7 – Identity by creating connections with others through the things they felt the most connected to in life.

And the doctor designed his PBR around #2 – Action, #8 – Intellectual Stimulation, and #10 – Making a Difference by passing on his skills and knowledge so that he had the greatest impact in his field of reach.

When you meet with traditional financial planners, you often come away with cut-and-dry plans to move your money around in ways that simply mitigate risk in retirement or improve the potential for better returns. There is not a lot of consideration for what you will do in retirement. You could make an argument that helping someone retire financially could be a disservice if that retiree will then feel listless and unfulfilled. Certainly, most financial planners are not starting with the big PURPOSE questions:

1. Do you want to stop working altogether or work on your own terms?

2. What day-to-day activities will make you happy and fulfilled in retirement?

3. Are you clear on the legacy you want your life savings to leave?

When I talk to clients about retirement, I always start with Purpose first. It is important to remember that the motivation behind your Purpose is not activities or actions. Motivation is what personally drives you. Your motivations are unique and personal to you. Your Purpose is intimately linked to these motivating drivers. Think of your motivation as internal and your Purpose as external. Your internal motivation drives your external actions or purpose. When you can identify what motivates you, then planning for your retirement becomes less scary.

A confident retirement starts with a true education about your risks and options to mitigate them, so you don't have to worry about what's around the corner next year. Up until this point in your life, the name of the game has been saving and investing and, let's honestly face it, outside of the hours you put in making that money in the first place, watching your money grow in the market hasn't been all that challenging.

That's all about to change. Preparing your finances (properly) for retirement is one of those things that is simple, but not easy— some of the biggest threats to our retirement confidence come from an emotional place, not necessarily a rational one. Your money motivations have changed. It's going to get much more difficult before it gets easier. If someone tries to tell you otherwise, they aren't looking out for anyone other than themselves.

When you begin planning for retirement with Purpose first and clearly identifiable motives, then organizing the four key factors in retirement becomes much easier.

People are increasingly able to retire younger and younger, and the options they have after retirement are now greater and greater. This is why *Job Optional** seemed like the perfect title to this book— with clear purpose and proper planning, the choice in how, when, and why you "retire" is yours.

CHAPTER 1: TAKEAWAYS, ACTIONS, AND NOTES

What are your biggest takeaways from this chapter?

_____

_____

_____

What are 3 action steps that you should work on now?

1. _____

2. _____

3. _____

What are 3 action steps for later?

1. _____

2. _____

3. _____

Notes:

_____

_____

_____

_____

_____

_____

PURPOSE-BASED ASSET ALLOCATION

Investing is a big factor when it comes to retirement, and many pre-retirees and retirees hyper-focus on it. It is my belief that you must look beyond investing and into areas such as higher taxes, gaps in health care coverage and inflation—these are the inefficiencies that, if left untreated, can drain your assets and leave fewer dollars in your pocket.

I refer to this as Purpose-Based Asset Allocation.[2]

Most of the time, meeting with a financial advisor is like running into a local pharmacy to fix a cold. You're prescribed an over-the-counter medication after a 10-minute consultation without regard to the real problem. Now, if it's just a cold, maybe your quick visit fixed your issue, but when it comes to your retirement, we're not facing a minor illness, but instead a major ailment with many accompanying risks.

Your financial doctor will need to take significant preparations, just as you may take for a knee surgery or something as serious as heart surgery.

Before my wife had knee surgery, we had several consultations with general practitioners and specialists. They didn't just prescribe the knee surgery, but took their time in identifying the issue and the ultimate treatment. They even took her blood pressure and heart rate, which you may think are unrelated, but the potential risks from not checking these things as well as medical history could result in death.

I would argue the same is true for your retirement planning. The risks are broad, and without taking into consideration all factors, you could overlook something, putting your financial health at risk. Real financial planning takes everything into account before any "medications" are ultimately prescribed. This is not only going to allow your planner to recommend the most appropriate strategies for your retirement but will also allow you to understand why they are making those recommendations in the first place. I find the better we understand the rationale behind a decision, the more confident we are that we have made a good one and, as a result, this allows us to live a more confident retirement.

Do You Know Where Your Money Is?

Many retirees just have a pile of money invested in various ways they don't understand. I met some who have multiple advisors and dozens of accounts—many working against one another.

MEET DENNIS AND KAREN

Years ago, I met the sweetest couple, Dennis and Karen, who were truly hard workers, not only in their careers but in their personal lives, as well. They had biological children in their younger years but, when they found they couldn't have any more, they set out to adopt. They had planned to adopt a healthy child, but one day Dennis was confronted with a seemingly difficult decision. A special needs baby had come up for adoption. He immediately called Karen and said if they didn't adopt her, then who would? Without skipping a beat, Karen said to bring the baby home, knowing this would be a lifetime commitment and they would be taking care of this child into their golden years. This was just the kind of people they were, some of the hardest working and caring individuals I know. Along the way, they were always focused on how to earn more, cover their expenses, and find a little extra to put away for retirement.

However, problems were evident. They would go from one investment to the next as they changed jobs. They had recommendations from friends and met with various advisors over the years. Each presented them with the next shiny object to resolve their financial woes and get them to retirement. And, as busy as they were between their careers and taking care of their children, there was little time left over for planning for retirement.

When I met Dennis and Karen, I walked into the conference room to greet them and saw some of the other chairs in the room were filled with a briefcase and a couple of grocery bags. It turned out the briefcase and those grocery bags were full of investment and insurance statements from all the "shiny objects" they had been sold over the years.

They didn't know how much money they had, where it was or what it was doing for them. They didn't feel they had enough for retirement, and they realized they didn't have a plan. This caused them stress and could have been the cause of various ailments they had suffered over the years.

Dennis and Karen had variable annuities for which they paid fees for benefits they would never use. They had mutual funds with expenses that could have been eliminated years prior. They had life insurance policies for which they were either overpaying or that had convoluted death benefit requirements for which they would never qualify. They were paying unnecessary taxes on after-tax benefits. They had no beneficiaries listed on many of their accounts, and, perhaps most importantly of all, they had no idea how much money they really had, let alone an estate plan to ensure their special needs daughter would be taken care of after they were gone.

Many of these products and investments were working against each other through portfolio overlap and misaligned benefits. It ended up taking us years to uncover all the different places they had stuffed away money. Just about every time they came in to review their assets, they brought in a new statement that had come in the mail from some unexpected and long-forgotten asset.

Once we determined exactly what they had and where it was, we could finally organize it toward their common purpose in retirement. Once Dennis and Karen had cut their unnecessary expenses and aligned their investments with their true goals, they had nearly double the assets they thought they did and were finally ready to put the financial worries and stress of the rat race behind them. They retired to spend time with their children and previously neglected hobbies; they finally started taking care of themselves the way they should have years prior.

Liability vs Purpose-Based Planning

How can you have peace of mind without specifically identifying the unique risks your retirement will face and how each one of your assets will address them?

Liability-Driven Planning

The definition of Liability-Driven Planning is when you have already created the asset and the only things that can take it away are the liabilities you will potentially face. In my experience, along the way, uncertainty regarding the future often leads people to inappropriate investments and unnecessary stresses due to their desire to preserve assets against undefined liabilities.

> THE BIGGEST MISTAKES I HAVE SEEN RETIREES MAKE ARE DUE TO NOT HAVING A PLAN FOR THEIR POTENTIAL RISKS OR LIABILITIES WHEN THEY ARISE, LEADING TO PANIC.

Purposed-Based Planning

Purpose-Based Asset Allocation is defined as the actions taken when you identify the specific risks you will face, assess how each one of these risks will affect you and allocate your assets to most efficiently defend against them, systematically starting with the most important. Most simply, the purpose of your assets is four-fold: liquidity, income, growth, and estate planning.

Regardless of the planning style, all retirees face unique risks for their unique situations, but most will face four basic risks, to varying degrees.

1. Emergencies requiring - Liquidity

2. Expenses requiring - Income

3. Inflation requiring - Growth

4. Death and ailments requiring - Estate planning

You will face unknown emergencies during retirement, requiring liquidity to fund them, including things like:

- Market corrections, maybe even crashes, jeopardizing the reliability of your retirement income

- Longevity risk or the risk of outliving your retirement savings

- Rising taxes, reducing your annual income and the assets you plan to leave behind

- Inflation pressures, reducing the purchasing power of your spendable income

- Major health care expenses, placing an undue burden on loved ones

> YOU WILL FACE UNKNOWN EMERGENCIES DURING RETIREMENT, REQUIRING LIQUIDITY TO FUND THEM.

Maximizing Your Efficiency

My middle school cross-country coach was a dry man, but full of wisdom in the little things he said. At every practice and before every meet, he would tell us to remember that the shortest distance between two points was a straight line. In running, it meant to stay on the inside track instead of taking the long way around on corners.

In retirement, the same concept applies: inefficiencies in your portfolio may not completely prevent you from achieving your financial goals, but they sure won't help you attain your goals faster.

Many of the retirees we meet with have their entire retirement in a portfolio of mutual funds, which they are relying on for a lifetime of retirement income. They keep the entire portfolio of funds in an overly conservative allocation, as they never know when a market pullback will come, and they can't suffer a huge loss on the whole portfolio. If instead, we can reposition a portion of the portfolio to satisfy retirement income needs over a pre-determined period of years, we then buy back our youth, in a sense.

> A MUTUAL FUND IS AN INVESTMENT VEHICLE THAT IS MADE UP OF A POOL OF FUNDS COLLECTED FROM MANY INVESTORS FOR THE PURPOSE OF INVESTING IN SECURITIES SUCH AS STOCKS, BONDS, MONEY MARKET INSTRUMENTS AND SIMILAR ASSETS. MUTUAL FUNDS ARE OPERATED BY MONEY MANAGERS WHO INVEST THE FUND'S CAPITAL AND ATTEMPT TO PRODUCE CAPITAL GAINS AND INCOME FOR THE FUND'S INVESTORS.

How's that? If we have better protections and lower risk for a portion of our portfolio, that means we can take more risk investing and achieve greater long-term returns in the overall portfolio with the remaining assets. We can invest our earmarked assets more in line with the way we did when we were younger. Why? Because we have an anti-anxiety pill to fall back on and satisfy income needs in a down market.

A gentleman who visited with our team reflected a product-specific example of an inefficient retirement plan. He had all his retirement savings invested in a variable annuity from a policy purchased years prior. He wanted out of the annuity, but could not exit, in his mind, because of a large death benefit rider on the policy. When we evaluated the cost of the death benefit rider, we found we could pay the same premium to a life insurance carrier and get a substantially larger tax-free death benefit than he would get as a taxable death benefit in his annuity. In addition, we could reposition the funds inside the annuity into an investment portfolio that would cut his fees and expenses in half, unleashing the growth power of his savings. Unleashing the efficiency of your life savings requires specifically identifying the specific purpose AND having the right tools in place to accomplish them.

Identifying Risks To Maximize Efficiency

Retirees have always faced the same general risks. However, these risks have evolved over time and so must your strategies; otherwise, it's akin to driving down the highway looking in the rearview mirror.

I was once given a pointer about keeping the future in focus:

"You must recognize there is a reason your front windshield is bigger than the rearview mirror—the most important part of preparing for the future is recognizing that it lies in front of you."

Risk 1: Interest Rates

Depending on your age, you may have a different reaction to the concept of "interest rates." Chances are, if you are reading this book and preparing for retirement, you'll recall the rate of return you could get on a certificate of deposit (CD) back in the 1980s, or even just 10 or 20 years ago. In 1981, the peak of interest rates in modern history, even a three-month CD could pay 14 percent interest. As recently as 2002, my dad purchased a fixed annuity[3] paying a guaranteed seven percent in interest annually for ten years.

If you could get a 7 percent guaranteed interest rate, odds are you wouldn't be reading this book. Higher guaranteed interest rates could solve a multitude of risks you will face in retirement—granted, they wouldn't solve *all* your risks, as you would still face such things as taxes and healthcare expenses, but normalizing interest rates would greatly improve your financial efficiency overall.

Stocks, bonds and cash used to be the foundation of all financial strategies. Nowadays, with interest rates at all-time lows at the time I am writing this book, bonds are paying less interest and facing price pressures when interest rates do begin to rise. Cash is paying next to nothing, at least not enough to keep up with inflation, and then we come to the stock or equity portion of your portfolio.

Just a quick look at the following chart will show why stocks are touted as the best way to get a leg up on inflation, but stocks come with their own drawbacks.

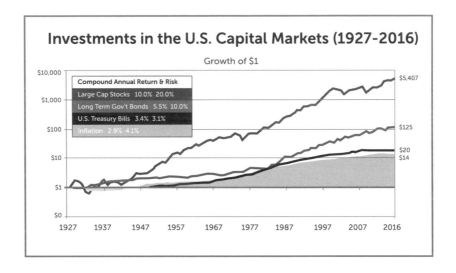

Risk 2: Stock Market Volatility

Regardless of the current valuation of the market, there are always unknown and unforeseen risks to equities or stocks traded on public exchanges. You may have heard your broker or advisor say the stock market averages 6 to 10 percent per year, so why would you put your money anywhere else?

While there is some merit to these words of advice, you aren't getting the whole picture. Saying the stock market averages 6 to 10 percent per year is like me saying my wife and I run an average of 30 miles per week—but I only jog two of them. The reality is, the stock market doesn't make these returns in a linear fashion. This is what we call volatility (ups and downs/roller coaster rides).

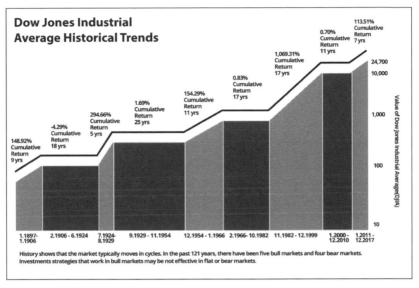

Source: https://www.risadvisory.com/images/uploads/Rydex_Historical_trends.pdf

In this chart you can see that the market goes through two types of periods, expansion and contraction, also known as bull and bear markets. Even though the long-term average has been very strong, the reality is there are periods of time extending years, even decades, where you would have experienced little to no return.

These periods of bear markets and/or volatility can not only lead to losses in equities, but also in the fixed income portion of your portfolio. When the stock market as a whole is losing ground, such as during a recession, even investments you thought of as consistent or reliable will lose value, even those tried-and-true assets like bonds, blue chip stocks, or dividend-paying stocks. This wasn't a problem during your working career, as you didn't need the money. If you were making periodic deposits to your investments out of your paycheck, you would purchase more quantities of asset classes that were depressed in value and less when they were overvalued, effectively allowing you to time the market without having to know anything about it. This is what is known as dollar-cost averaging[4], a fantastic strategy that all should employ while saving for retirement.

The following chart shows what this dollar-cost averaging can look like. The column for Account #1 represents an account that purchases $1,000 of shares each month. If the stock value is up, the account purchases fewer. If stock values are down, the account purchases more. Compare that valuation with Account #2, where an initial $5,000 purchased 250 shares.

DOLLAR-COST AVERAGING

Account #1: $1,000 monthly contributions		VS	Account #2: a one-time $5,000 contribution (250 shares)	
Month	Share Price	Shares Bought	Account #1 Value	Account #2 Value
January	$20	50	$ 1,000	$ 5,000
February	$16	63	$ 1,800	$ 4,000
March	$12	83	$ 2,350	$ 3,000
April	$17	59	$ 4,329	$ 4,250
May	$23	43	$ 6,857	$ 5,750

(This is a hypothetical example that is demonstrating a mathematical principle. It does not illustrate any investment products and does not show past or future performance of any specific investment.)

The opposite is true as your needs change in retirement from accumulation to deaccumulation. Retirees often say they are out of time when they get to retirement. Why? Because you are going to have immediate needs for a portion of your funds that you didn't have prior, called cash flow. As you begin taking distributions from your portfolio, the market will inevitably go down, or at least some of the assets in your portfolio, and if income is indiscriminately taken from these investments, you will be violating the No. 1 rule of investing: "Buy low and sell high."

This is what put many retirees back to work following the dot-com bust and the financial crisis of 2008. If you were working, these down markets presented the opportunity to purchase cheap assets and let them rebound, but in retirement you faced quite the opposite.

These potential losses present the greatest risk at the front end of your retirement. You can afford losses during your retirement, but you cannot afford severe losses on the front end. In other words, you may experience a market that averages eight percent per year and, if the good returns are at the front end with the bad on the back, you're OK. Flip those returns and with the same average rate of return? You may run out of funds during retirement. Simply saying "I only need to average 6 percent per year in retirement" and "I've done better in the past" doesn't work—this is what is called sequence of returns risk. When interviewed on the *Retirement with Purpose* podcast, Professor of Retirement Income at The American College, Dr. Wade Pfau, had this to say about sequence of returns risk: "the stock market on average earns 7 percent after inflation, so 7 percent should be a safe withdrawal rate with 100 percent stock and unfortunately, that's not how things work…The idea of sequence of returns risk and the amount you can spend in retirement might be less than what you think based on the average market returns over that (your specific) retirement period."

Following are charts depicting different risks encountered by two retirees. Steve retired in 1990 and enjoyed appreciable gains following one down year at the beginning of retirement. Bill retired in 2000 and experienced three years of unfavorable returns at the beginning of retirement. Overall, the two men will likely face the same "average" return in retirement, but their account values will be very different depending on the order of their returns, and whether losses occurred earlier or later in retirement.

Income and Sequence of Returns

Steve | Retired in 1990

End of Year	Market Return[1]	Withdrawal	IRA Account Balance
1990	-4.34%	$ 30,000	$ 449,602
1991	20.32%	$ 30,000	$ 504,865
1992	4.17%	$ 30,000	$ 494,667
1993	13.72%	$ 30,000	$ 528,419
1994	2.14%	$ 30,000	$ 509,085
1995	33.45%	$ 30,000	$ 639,340
1996	26.01%	$ 30,000	$ 767,829
1997	22.64%	$ 30,000	$ 904,873
1998	16.10%	$ 30,000	$ 1,015,728
1999	25.22%	$ 30,000	$ 1,234,328

Income and Sequence of Returns

Bill | Retired in 2000

End of Year	Market Return[1]	Withdrawal	IRA Account Balance
2000	-6.18%	$ 30,000	$ 440,954
2001	-7.10%	$ 30,000	$ 381,776
2002	-16.76%	$ 30,000	$ 292,819
2003	25.32%	$ 30,000	$ 329,364
2004	3.15%	$ 30,000	$ 308,794
2005	-0.61%	$ 30,000	$ 277,094
2006	16.29%	$ 30,000	$ 287,345
2007	6.43%	$ 30,000	$ 273,892
2008	-33.84%	$ 30,000	$ 161,359
2009	18.82%	$ 30,000	$ 156,081

(These are hypothetical examples demonstrating a mathematical principle. They do not illustrate any investment products and do not show past or future performance of any specific investment.)

Risk 3: Longevity and Health Care Costs

The longer you live, the higher the probability you will face market crashes or corrections and, today, retirees are living longer than ever. This probably won't change, either. With advances in medical technology and our country's renewed focus on healthy eating and exercise, someone retiring at the age of 60 may spend more time in retirement than they did working. Prominent author, lecturer, and founder of Edelman Financial Services, Ric Edelman, spoke on this topic, saying, "Your clients are going to live to 120, and if you haven't built that into your financial plan, you're not running accurate projections for them."

This means you will face a higher probability of not only running out of money in retirement, but also higher potential health care costs in addition to a rising cost of living. The longer you live, the more you are affected by inflation.

In addition, health care costs have historically seen much higher rates of inflation than other expenses you will face in retirement. You may think to yourself, "I am in great shape and take excellent care of myself, not to mention my genealogy," but those exact things may be what lead to higher health care costs as you live longer than those around you.

My wife, for instance, comes from a large family with multiple generations. Not only is her gene pool better than mine, but she's in great health. At her age, her great-great-grandmother was very similar. As a matter of fact, at the time I am writing this book, she is still in fantastic health at age 100. However, her mind isn't cooperating, and she has spent the last decade in a nursing home, incurring average monthly costs of over $5,000.

This is a risk often overlooked when planning for the retirement of a couple. On average, men have little chance of outliving our female counterparts and, if statistics become reality, overlooking the continuation of retirement for a surviving spouse could be extremely detrimental.

Furthermore, I am afraid, due to our aging population and with nearly 10,000 people turning 65 every day, the costs of health care aren't going down anytime soon.

A surviving spouse will see a loss of income, a greater impact of inflation, higher probability of market volatility, increased taxes as a single-filer, and a greater risk of long-term care expenses because they no longer have a spouse to rely on. These are just a few of the risks a surviving spouse will face that cannot be overlooked when structuring a solid retirement plan for TWO.

"...80 percent of men die married, 80 percent of women die widowed...70 percent to 80 percent of women will leave the financial advisor that they're working with right now if their husband dies within 18 months and the reason is the financial advisor is not working closely with them. The financial advisor's always been working with the husband."

~David Bach,
Smart Women Finish Rich: 9 Steps to Achieving Financial Security and Funding Your Dreams

LIKELIHOOD OF A 65-YEAR-OLD LIVING TO AGE...

	Male - Single	Female - Single	At least one member of a couple
85	41%	53%	72%
90	20%	32%	45%
95	6%	13%	18%

Source: https://personal.vanguard.com/us/insights/retirement/plan-for-a-long-retirement-tool?lang=en

Risk 4: Inflation Risks

The monetary stimulus seen from central banks around the world may affect our rates of inflation in the short-term, which means we will all inevitably face some form of inflation in the future.

Just ask yourself this question, what did you pay for your first home? Now what did you pay for your last car? If you've been around long enough, you will find those numbers may be strikingly close together. That's inflation.

The longer your retirement, the higher the likelihood you will face some effects of inflation. Without a strategy for increasing your income throughout retirement, you may be left with half of the purchasing power you had at the onset of retirement thirty years in—or worse.

Efficiency

Have you ever been to Mexico or the Caribbean, and experienced one of those amphibious boat rides? My wife and I did. The attraction was called the "Amazing Amphibious Bus Tour." The Cayman Islands, located in the British West Indies, are known for clear blue water, powdery white sand beaches, and great places for snorkeling. For our one-year anniversary, we decided to purchase tickets to ride on what looks like a large bus with gigantic windows that tours the city of George Town one minute and splashes into turquoise water the next. It was a fun trip and an interesting ride, but there are tradeoffs to riding in a vehicle that does double duty as both a boat and a bus. As clever and entertaining as our tour guide was, he could do little about the fact that the bus was slow. He could also not improve our comfort level. Even though the boat was labeled "unsinkable" because of the strategic insertion of foam in sections of the bus/ boat's undercarriage, we were still afloat in a road vehicle that, for all the reassurance given us by our driver/captain, seemed unseaworthy.

The amphibious bus, or hydra/terra, as some call it, reminds me of the financial strategies put in place by some financial advisors these days. Attempts to cobble together strategies that give you the best of both worlds often miss the mark completely.

Variable annuities are often touted as the silver bullet for retirees. They offer market participation for inflation protection, guaranteed income riders you cannot outlive, and even death benefits for your loved ones after you're gone. The reality is that these elements come at a price, which often exceeds 4 percent per year. The end result is less growth for inflation protection than what is available in other market products, less guaranteed income than alternative guaranteed income products with a single focus, and a taxable death benefit that comes at a higher cost than a tax-free life insurance policy.

> A VARIABLE ANNUITY IS A TYPE OF ANNUITY CONTRACT THAT ALLOWS FOR THE ACCUMULATION OF CAPITAL ON A TAX-DEFERRED BASIS. IT OFFERS INVESTORS THE OPPORTUNITY TO GENERATE HIGHER RATES OF RETURNS BY INVESTING IN EQUITY AND BOND SUBACCOUNTS.

I also commonly see retirees retire with a big "diversified" portfolio of stocks and bonds, or more likely mutual funds and exchange-traded funds[5], expecting this to cover all their retirement risks.

If you're relying on this portfolio to be your emergency fund, what happens if it's down 20 percent and an emergency strikes? How will you avoid selling when the market is down if you need to meet your monthly income requirements? How will it generate enough income to meet your health care expenses if you suddenly have a long-term care demand? These are just a few of the reasons you will need to use different assets to accomplish each of your specific goals. Otherwise, you are missing the full potential of covering each one. Clearly identify the purpose of each asset and you will be well on your way to reaching your goal in a straight line of efficiency.

For more on this topic, check out the Educational Videos section of the Howard Bailey website and watch our video, "A Brief Lesson on Alternative Investments":

https://howardbailey.com/educational-videos/iul/

Mind Off My Money, Money Off My Mind

The ultimate goal of structuring a solid financial plan for retirement is to have matters settled. I want you to answer this question for yourself: "What does retirement mean to me?"

I know at first it may seem like a silly question, but I have asked that question to literally thousands of retirees and pre-retirees and the answers vary widely from freedom, to time with family, to pursuit of neglected interests. I have never had anyone answer "money." However, in every instance, I met these individuals and discussed specific concerns regarding money, either at a live seminar event or in my office.

I hope to make this the last financial book you read during retirement, so you can stop thinking about money and truly begin enjoying your retirement to the fullest.

For decades, you have been focused on accumulating money and, with the right plan, you can fulfill the true purpose of having the money in the first place, which is to fund your ability to do the other things that are important to you.

This cannot be accomplished if your plan is dependent on the stock market to do well year in and year out. A plan based on constant best-case scenarios isn't much of a plan. A Purpose-Based Plan will not only allow you to identify a fulfilling purpose for retirement but will also allow you to live out that purpose without worry. Of course, you may never be able to eliminate all your retirement concerns or risks, but with a real plan, at least we can cover the ones that are most identifiable and play defense against the unknown, then you can decide what is most important to you.

CHAPTER 2: TAKEAWAYS, ACTIONS, AND NOTES

What are your biggest takeaways from this chapter?

_____

_____

_____

What are 3 action steps that you should work on now?

1. _____

2. _____

3. _____

What are 3 action steps for later?

1. _____

2. _____

3. _____

Notes:

_____

_____

_____

_____

_____

_____

LIQUIDITY PLANNING

What if your adult child must move back in with you? What if your best friend wins an exotic trip and you get an invite to tag along? What if you have a major unexpected repair to your car? What if the Europe trip you've dreamed of comes up at an unexpected discount, but earlier than you budgeted for?

Whether it's an opportunity or something less fortunate, certain life happenings come at us quickly, and if you don't have liquidity money in the bank, so to speak—you may be forced to forego opportunities or, worse, put them on a high-interest credit card.

Be Ready for the Unexpected

Studies have shown it's not those who have more income or more investments or even more net worth who are the happiest and most financially secure.

Instead, those who are happiest possess the largest bank balances with cash readily available in the case of emergency. I have found this to be especially true for retirees, due to the lessened financial flexibility provided by a fixed income.

You can no longer pick up a little extra overtime to fund those unexpected events. You're on your own. A rock-solid financial plan is your only option. Now, I am not suggesting you liquidate all investments and shift them into a bank account, but I am suggesting you ensure that you have an adequate emergency fund prior to stepping into retirement.

What that means to you may be different from the next person because any definitive amount is dependent on a couple of factors. At a minimum, we suggest you have at least six months' worth of your expenses put away in a bank account, easily accessed in case the need arises. In some cases, we have liquidated investments or extended a retirement date to raise the funds; it's that important. Beyond that, the "right amount" is whatever helps you sleep at night, but only if it doesn't jeopardize your overall financial plan.

I have some clients who will set aside one to two years' worth of expenses to feel secure. In that case, you may want to look at alternatives to traditional banking products such as savings accounts, money markets, or certificates of deposit. A conservative investment portfolio may make sense for a portion of these funds or even a properly structured insurance product.

I myself keep the funds needed to pay off our home mortgage in an overfunded cash value life insurance policy. I maintain my mortgage interest deduction and defer my annual gains inside of my life insurance policy, which, if never needed, will pass on tax-free to my heirs. I can also use the death benefit while I am living through an accelerated death benefit rider, providing some protection in the case of my disability or long-term care need.

In addition, I am averaging a higher net rate of return than what I pay on my mortgage balance. It's important to note: For this to work, you need to have the policy structured in such a way as to ensure you can't lose your original investment and there are no penalties for early withdrawal.

I once had a client with an old life insurance policy they had funded for more than twenty years (getting them well past any surrender charges), from which they were netting annual returns of 4 percent per year, which, at the time, was substantially better than they could get at the bank. They moved funds from their bank account into the life insurance policy, dramatically increasing the annual returns on what they viewed as their emergency fund and increasing their death benefits as well. Remember, if they never leverage the death benefit for "living benefits," then the value will pass tax-free to their heirs.

If you don't have a life insurance policy that has passed the surrender charge period, you may want to establish what is known as a modified endowment contract (MEC), essentially overfunding a life insurance policy and waiving the surrender charges to ensure protection of the cash value, growth and liquidity in the case of emergency. If a policy becomes a MEC, it will be treated as a non-qualified annuity for tax purposes.

This is another example of maximizing the efficiency of your hard-earned life savings. The bottom line: Have an emergency fund, regardless of the size, so you know you can cover those unknown events during retirement.

CHAPTER 3: TAKEAWAYS, ACTIONS, AND NOTES

What are your biggest takeaways from this chapter?

_____

_____

_____

What are 3 action steps that you should work on now?

1. _____

2. _____

3. _____

What are 3 action steps for later?

1. _____

2. _____

3. _____

Notes:

_____

_____

_____

_____

_____

_____

CHAPTER FOUR

INCOME PLANNING

Without income, there cannot be retirement. There may not be a more important part of your retirement strategy than a comprehensive income plan that covers longevity, market and tax risks. Simply setting a goal for a certain rate of return and regular distributions is not a retirement income strategy. Neither is generating enough dividends and interest to live off without touching the principal. Let me explain why it's much more than that.

> A RATE OF RETURN (ROR) IS THE NET GAIN OR LOSS ON AN INVESTMENT OVER A SPECIFIED TIME PERIOD, EXPRESSED AS A PERCENTAGE OF THE INVESTMENT'S INITIAL COST.

The 4 Percent Withdrawal Rule

Also known as The Prudent Man's Rule, the 4 Percent Withdrawal Rule was pioneered by a California-based financial advisor named William Bengen in 1994. It was then popularized by "The Trinity Study" in 1998, and later titled SAFEMAX for the maximum "safe" historical withdrawal rate. The idea is that retirees investing in a portfolio split between stocks and bonds could withdraw 4 percent from that portfolio in the first year of retirement. Then, the retirees could make inflation-adjusted withdrawals in subsequent years over a thirty-year retirement and most likely not deplete their savings (the key there being "most likely"). Bengen used historical data dating to 1926. However, some things have changed, and many economists and professors of finance are questioning whether this rule still stands, given the evolving economic environment of today.

Without diving too deep into statistics, the bottom line is that a retiree doesn't get a significant amount of confidence regarding their retirement when there is any chance of total failure. Even if we can illustrate a 95 percent chance of success, that 5 percent chance of failure could happen tomorrow if you retire at the peak of a market, before a major stock market correction or even crash. In the end, using any set of purely market-based investments with an accompanying scheduled withdrawal rate is not a plan for the worst, but instead a plan that is hoping for the best and planning for the best. Instead, you should be planning for the best and preparing for the worst.

Interest-Only Income Strategy

Another popular strategy relies on generating enough dividends or interest to cover any monthly retirement income needs. Similar to the concept of a 4 percent withdrawal, this strategy depends largely on markets consistently performing well. Yet, the most glaring problem here is most retirees haven't saved enough to adequately live off the interest income from their investments. The average 60-something has around $150,000 saved for retirement. Even if you could generate a 6 percent return for annual income, you would only create $1,000 per month in pre-tax income, whereas the average retired household in the U.S. has roughly $3,500 in after-tax expenses.

In many instances, when a client pushes their advisor to achieve these rates of yield on their investments, they end up taking on excessive degrees of risk using high-yield (also known as junk) bonds, long-term bonds, oil and gas partnerships, real estate investment trusts, or even unstable high-yielding stocks. Even so, the highest quality large cap stocks may cut or even eliminate their dividends in a down market, and your bonds may default altogether. This is just another buy-and-hope approach, lending an equal degree of uncertainty to your retirement as the 4 Percent Withdrawal Rule.

Real Income Strategies

There is no one-size-fits-all approach when it comes to implementing an income strategy for your retirement years. Some annuity pushers may tell you to guarantee all your lifetime income in retirement, while your securities broker might say you need to live off municipal bonds or dividend income.

The reality is, you must decide after you are presented with all the options. Each option has its own pros and cons. Since we've already mentioned guaranteed lifetime income, which may sound overwhelmingly appealing, why don't we start there?

Guaranteed Lifetime Income

The word "guarantee" can strike fear into the hearts of a retiree, just as much as the word "annuity."

There is valid reason to be concerned, too. In recent decades, we have seen a proliferation of financial scams and Ponzi schemes typically carrying such a word in their marketing pitches.

If you are being promised outlandish returns without the risk of principal losses, then yes, be afraid. Be very afraid.

However, if this word is being used in relation to the insurance world instead of the investment world, there may be validity to these guarantees[6]. The downside will most likely be the lack of long-term growth and flexibility in contrast to the world of investments. In return, you will receive guarantees that a stock broker will never be able to match, which may be worth some tradeoffs; it's up to you.

How Safe Is That "Guarantee," Really?

There is little opportunity for true guarantees in this world. As the saying goes, "the only thing in life that is guaranteed is death and taxes." Annuity guarantees, however, are about as close as it gets in the world of finance. Understanding how insurance companies are allowed to even use this word comes down to something known as the "legal reserve system".

The legal reserve system requires by law that certain levels of funds be set aside and maintained at all times to cover future obligations of the issuing company. The Federal Deposit Insurance Corporation (FDIC) is one example of a legal reserve system for banks, requiring them to have certain minimum guaranteed reserves available to satisfy their financial obligations. Some legal reserve systems require one hundred percent reserves (dollar-for-dollar) to be kept in place. Other systems may require only a few pennies on each dollar of obligations. Certificates of deposit, for instance, are backed by the legal federal reserves maintained by the FDIC. While the FDIC backs deposits up to $250,000 per Social Security number per institution, banks aren't required to keep 100 percent dollar-for-dollar legal reserves on hand to back up these deposits. Investments, such as stocks and bonds, don't carry reserve requirements, and that's one reason you may have seen some stocks and corporate bonds become completely worthless throughout history.

Savings vehicles backed by a legal reserve system include banks, government bonds and insurance companies. We've discussed banks and understand that the Federal Reserve can print its own money to back up government bonds, but how does an insurance company's legal reserve system operate?

The easiest way to describe this is to compare the way they operate with the way the banking system works. Banks are required by the Board of Governors of the Federal Reserve System (FRB) to keep a fraction of a dollar on hand for every dollar they lend.[7] This is what led to the financial crisis of 2008. We cannot say banks are not safe, as they are still backed by the FDIC and the government is able to quickly hit the printing presses to fill this gap.

I'm not saying banks aren't a secure place to put your money, but it's interesting to compare banks with insurance companies and which ones are on the most solid footing when it comes to required reserves.

The states, rather than the federal government, regulate insurance companies. What significance does that have? Insurance companies are required by law to follow the guidelines of up to fifty states versus one federal entity, if they intend to operate nationally, that is.[8] This fact tends to make them more regulated, not less. Unlike banks, insurance companies must have dollar-for-dollar in reserves. In addition, while banks are allowed to invest their working capital in a wide range of investments from mortgages to business loans, insurance companies are required to keep the majority of their customer's funds in ultra-conservative investments, such as U.S. government bonds, and highly rated corporate bonds. If they make more speculative investments, they must use their own capital, not the portion that is required by law to be set aside to settle potential customer claims.

The National Organization of Life and Health Insurance (NOLHGA) has stated that the fixed insurance industry is now better prepared than other areas of the financial industry to withstand national economic challenges, and that in the eighteen months leading up to June 2009, not a single life insurer had to be liquidated as a result of the economic downturn. Furthermore, there has not been a single failure of a fixed insurance carrier of national significance since 1994. This is in stark contrast to the sixty-two bank failures from 2008 to June 2009.[9][10]

Beyond its primary reserves, an insurance company further reduces risk through the use, and requirement of, surplus capital. Throughout my professional career, I've found most insurance companies hold somewhere between 5 percent and 15 percent in excess reserves. I've even seen companies in excess of 50 percent, or $150 on hand for every $100 they owe. When the surplus capital drops below minimums required by the state in which the company is located, the state may put the insurance company into receivership and take over. This is rare, but it has happened. When it does, the state takes over the legal responsibility to make sure client funds are transferred to a stronger insurance company as soon as possible. Client accounts of an insurance company are highly valuable, which is why, in most cases, a stronger insurance company is very willing to pay money and acquire those assets. What happens in the rare case where no buyer can be found to take over those assets and liabilities? This is when reinsurers step into the picture.

Reinsurance is the process by which part or all of the insurer's risk is assumed by other insurance companies in return for part of the premium paid by the insurer. Many primary insurers have purchased reinsurance from as many as 10 different companies. Despite all these safety nets being in place, it is still prudent to carry out your due diligence when placing your assets with an insurance company. Focus on the assets and investment of the insurance company before depositing your hard-earned dollars with them.

> **I HAVE NEVER HEARD A RETIREE SAY THEY HATE THEIR PENSION.**

I have never heard one of those retirees say they hate their pension. The reality is, their pension is just another form of an annuity. An annuity is an investment vehicle utilized by insurance companies to provide investment options, including a potential income stream. There are many different types of annuities, which may offer guaranteed income options—we will cover most of those here. Retirees' pensions (and their subsequent funding liability) used to land on the back of the employer.

Since the introduction of defined-contribution plans, such as 401(k)s, today's truth is you must create your own version of the pension yesterday's retirees enjoyed.

This is one of the biggest hurdles of today's retirement: You have focused on the growth and return on your money for decades, and you must now shift that focus to income and the return of your money. There will be trade-offs when it comes to flexibility and the long-term return of your assets

"More dangerous yet is the shift in focus away from retirement income to return on investment that has come with the introduction of saver-managed DC plans: Investment decisions are now focused on the value of the funds, the returns on investment they deliver, and how volatile those returns are. Yet the primary concern of the saver remains what it always has been: Will I have sufficient income in retirement to live comfortably?"

~Harvard Business Review, *The Crisis in Retirement Planning*[11]

regarding annuities. However, I have found over the years that many retirees are not as concerned with what they might leave behind as they are with having certainty on their returns. One difficulty is that many people lump all annuities into one category, immediate annuities, which are just one very small subset of a much larger category.

Immediate Annuity

An **immediate annuity**, also known as a single premium immediate annuity (SPIA), is a vehicle in which you make a lump sum deposit. As a result, you receive an income stream that could be structured to provide income over a specified period, or even a lifetime or two. This is a double-edged sword. You have a total loss of control over the lump sum, and the insurance company keeps whatever funds are left in the contract in the event of your early death. BUT—if the annuity covers you (or even you and your spouse) for a lifetime, you may outlive the amount of money you used to fund the contract, and the insurance company will continue your payments.

In a low-interest rate environment or a period of high inflation, you may of course be locked into an income that is disadvantageous. These vehicles may come in handy, though, if you have the goal of creating a period of guaranteed income of, say, five or ten years. This is especially the case with nonqualified or after-tax

AN IMMEDIATE ANNUITY, ALSO KNOWN AS AN INCOME OR SINGLE PREMIUM IMMEDIATE ANNUITY (SPIA), IS A CONTRACT BETWEEN YOU AND AN INSURANCE COMPANY DESIGNED FOR INCOME PURPOSES ONLY. UNLIKE A DEFERRED ANNUITY, AN IMMEDIATE ANNUITY SKIPS THE ACCUMULATION STAGE AND BEGINS PAYING OUT INCOME EITHER IMMEDIATELY OR WITHIN A YEAR AFTER YOU HAVE PURCHASED IT WITH A SINGLE, LUMP-SUM PAYMENT. SPIAS ARE ALSO CALLED IMMEDIATE PAYMENT ANNUITIES, INCOME ANNUITIES, LIFETIME ANNUITIES AND IMMEDIATE ANNUITIES.

funds, as the annuitization feature will allow you to spread out your taxable gain equally over the term of the contract. In addition, if you have selected a set period and pass away during the distribution period, the payments typically continue on to your heirs.

This is something my dad took advantage of with some of the nonqualified annuities he purchased over the years. He previously had fixed annuities, which he later transferred into fixed index annuities, and then annuitized years later to spread out the taxable gain that was deferred over the time he held those investments.

Utilizing a SPIA in such a way can buy you time to allow your at-risk investments to endure the continuing volatility of the stock market with much higher return potential.

Fixed Annuities

The next most basic form of an annuity is by far the easiest to understand—operating much like the familiar CD but backed by an insurance company instead of the FDIC or banking institution selling the product. A **fixed annuity** offers a fixed rate of return over a fixed period. Typically, the return is significantly higher than what would be offered through a bank product but accompanied with stiffer penalties for early withdrawal. Terms or surrender charge periods can vary over three- to ten-year periods, over which time you typically have some sort of penalty-free withdrawal in the amount of interest earned (or 5 to 10 percent of the account value).

A FIXED ANNUITY IS A TYPE OF ANNUITY CONTRACT THAT ALLOWS FOR THE ACCUMULATION OF CAPITAL ON A TAX-DEFERRED BASIS. IN EXCHANGE FOR A LUMP SUM OF CAPITAL, A LIFE INSURANCE COMPANY CREDITS THE ANNUITY ACCOUNT WITH A GUARANTEED FIXED INTEREST RATE WHILE GUARANTEEING THE PRINCIPAL INVESTMENT. A FIXED ANNUITY CAN BE ANNUITIZED TO PROVIDE THE ANNUITANT WITH A GUARANTEED INCOME PAYOUT FOR A SPECIFIED TERM OR FOR LIFE.

These products can make for a good alternative to an ultra-conservative CD, or even as a more secure alternative to the investment-grade bond market. I had many clients over the years who found these products to be a good fit for a large portion of their retirement savings for these reasons.

MEET BOB AND CHARLENE

Bob and Charlene came to my office after they encountered a significant level of frustration with their investments over the previous couple of years. They were strangers to the investment world. Their wealth was mostly made up of farmland that had been passed down for generations. Bob and Charlene had an interesting situation when they found their children were not interested in continuing the family legacy as farmers into the future. They decided to sell the farm. In addition, like many farmers—including those in my own family—this couple had very limited experiences outside of the farm. The demands of farming, for those of you who don't know, can be intense. Families on small farms wake up at the crack of dawn and often manage to get more done in the hours before the sun comes up than the average American can do in a day.

After Bob and Charlene sold their farm, they found a local investment broker who promised them higher returns than they had ever seen in the farming business. The proposal involved a blend of stock market and high-risk, limited-partnership-type investments. Two years after the initial sale of approximately half of their farmland, Bob and Charlene had seen ups and downs that left them with about 10 percent less in value than they started with—and this was during a strong bull market. They told me they never wanted to see their accounts go down in value again. They just couldn't take the stress.

Bob and Charlene never experienced the roller coaster runs of the market before, in contrast to the average 401(k) investors who have experienced multiple recessions over their lifetimes (and they may not have needed the risk, either). They were much like my father after he sold his apartments; he couldn't stomach losses on wealth that had taken so much energy to create.

Bob and Charlene could not handle traditional market-based investments but were ecstatic about a modest fixed rate that was guaranteed to credit interest to their account on a monthly basis without ever having to see the account dip in value.

The interest generated off their new fixed annuities more than covered their monthly expenses and allowed them to travel, experiencing things they could never have done had they held onto the farm. Furthermore, they may never have had the confidence to spend their money while it was fluctuating up and down in the stock market. Bob and Charlene continued to sell more of the farm and more farming equipment, opening more fixed annuities offering the certainty they wanted for their retirement years.

This wouldn't be the right fit for everyone, but it was the right fit for them, offering exactly the tool they were looking for in their retirement. Other individuals and retirees, on the other hand, are willing to accept a little volatility or lack of predictability with more upside potential than others.

Fixed Index Annuities

That leads us into our next major type of annuity, the **fixed index annuity**[12], which has grown dramatically in popularity over the last couple of decades. The fixed index annuity offers the principal guarantees of a fixed annuity with more upside potential closer to that offered in a traditional stock market investment. Returns are typically tied to some type of stock market index, such as the S&P 500, SPDR Gold Trust[13] or even actively managed indexes, after which, limits are put on annual returns. Returns can be limited in many ways, through such factors as participation rates, caps or spreads.

INDEXED ANNUITIES ARE INSURANCE CONTRACTS THAT, DEPENDING ON THE CONTRACT, MAY OFFER A GUARANTEED ANNUAL INTEREST RATE AND SOME PARTICIPATION IN A STOCK MARKET INDEX.

- A *participation rate* will offer a percentage of returns in whatever index it is tracking, such as 75 percent of the returns in the S&P 500 without downside risk.

- *Cap rates* limit returns to a specified percentage, such as 10 percent of the returns in the S&P 500 without downside risk.

- With *spreads*, also known as hurdles, your returns must exceed a certain percentage before you receive credits to your account, such as 2 percent per year, after which excess returns are credited to the client's account.

Arguably the most attractive aspect of a fixed index annuity is the periodic crediting—after which your contract locks in the increase in value of the account.

This can occur annually or maybe even as far out as every five years. On the other hand, any growth accrued over that period leading up to the lock-in date is earned and cannot be lost to downward market movements over the following lock-in term.

The primary downside of fixed index annuities is the same as the fixed annuity—you will be forced to take on some type of term with limited liquidity provisions. This could mean having a withdrawal limit of up to five to ten percent of the account value per year, or a contract term limit of five to 20 years.

The following charts illustrate how the "lock-in" provision of an FIA allows it to measure up against a stock market product, both in the short run or over a longer time period.

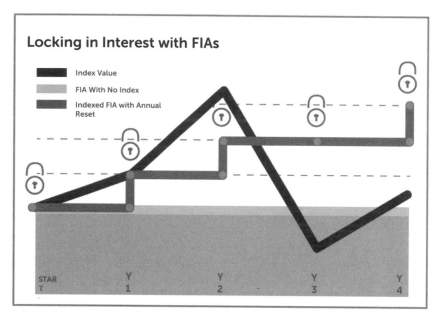

Source: https://www.allianzlife.com/~/media/files/global/documents/2016/05/18/08/18/m-5217.pdf

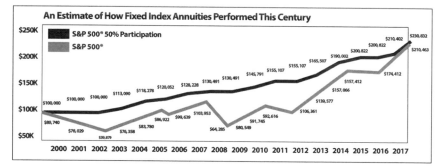

More information on this graph may be obtained in the End Notes section.[14]

Obviously, the more flexibility you are willing or able to give up, the more potential for interest credits you will be offered in return. Stock brokers most often cite the limited returns and flexibility these vehicles offer as the reason people shouldn't use them.

Over time, I found that many retirees aren't looking for stock-market-like returns anymore. Instead, they are seeking modest returns without the concern of losing half of their life savings in the market or facing obstacles such as bond defaults during retirement. My dad is one of those people, often saying he has saved enough for retirement and that he just needs to make 4 to 6 percent and not lose it. Most of his life savings are in various indexed products, from annuities to life insurance, offering him the principal protection he seeks and the growth potential that enables him to be content. Some of the people we have worked with over the years still want the guaranteed income offered through such things as SPIAs but want to maintain more flexibility and growth potential as well.

Fixed Index Annuities With A GLWB Rider

Some fixed index annuities may offer something called a **guaranteed lifetime withdrawal benefit rider**[15] (GLWB). You might think of riders as sidecars to the main event—you have all the principal protection and growth potential of a fixed index annuity, but the "sidecar" rider also puts income guarantees on top of your basic policy.

To understand this concept, think about it as a T-chart. On one side is what we call your "accumulation value," acting like the fixed index annuity we discussed earlier. I prefer to think of this side of the chart as your

A GUARANTEED LIFETIME WITHDRAWAL BENEFIT (GLWB) IS A RIDER TO AN ANNUITY CONTRACT THAT ALLOWS FOR LIFETIME GUARANTEED WITHDRAWALS TO BE MADE FROM AN ANNUITY DURING THE OWNER'S LIFETIME WITHOUT PENALTY. THE OWNER TYPICALLY PAYS FOR THE GLWB WITH AN EXTRA PERCENTAGE OF FEES OF THE TOTAL VALUE OF THE ANNUITY CONTRACT.

"real money". These are the funds you can walk away with after the surrender charge period, or which you can leave to your beneficiaries as a lump-sum death benefit.

The other side of the T-chart represents the value of a potential future income stream known as a Guaranteed Lifetime Withdrawal Benefit. The value of your GLWB rider can grow in various ways but will usually carry some type of enhanced growth benefit over what is offered on the accumulation value ("real money") side. It may come in the form of a guaranteed annual return rate; a multiple of interest credited to the accumulation value or a lock-in rate that occurs more regularly—as frequently as daily.

This rider side of your T-chart is a calculation of the amount of income your contract will guarantee for the rest of your life—typically expressed as a percentage dependent on the age of the owner or beneficiary of the account. The insurance company will use this to calculate the income checks they send to you, but should you choose to take your money out of the contract at the end of your surrender period, this is not the side of the T-chart that you can walk away with. Think about the potential of outliving your life savings. You insure your car and home, why not insure the biggest risk you face in retirement?

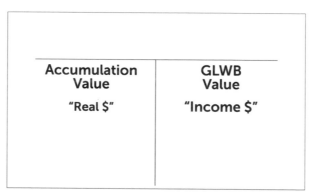

My mom had an annuity like this of her own purchased just prior to the financial collapse of 2008. She deposited her IRA value into an account where she was offered approximately 60 percent of the gains in the market, locked-in every two years (the left side of the T-chart). In addition, she added a GLWB rider, guaranteeing her an 8 percent annual rate of return on funds to be used for future retirement income (the right side of the T-chart).

As a result, not only did she never experience the 2008 losses to her principal, but her GLWB value grew at 8 percent compounded annually for future retirement income needs. At the age of sixty-five, she was guaranteed an annual withdrawal of 5 1/2 percent of the GLWB value per year for the rest of her life. As a teacher with a meager pension and spousal Social Security benefits, this offered her the ability to fill the gap in her expenses on a guaranteed basis without being concerned by the market volatility she may experience in her other investments.

Whatever she didn't spend would be left behind to me. Furthermore, since she funded it by rolling over some of her IRA, she didn't mind losing out on some flexibility—because of the tax implications of her traditional IRA, she was never going to take a large distribution from these funds and wasn't looking to them for liquidity.

MEET ROBERT AND CHERYL

I came across a couple, Robert and Cheryl, who were looking to purchase an immediate annuity to have a source of guaranteed income during their retirement years. They weren't sure when they would need to begin taking income during retirement. They were still enjoying their careers and didn't know exactly when they would retire.

Rather than stuffing them into an immediate annuity contract, which would immediately begin generating income they didn't yet need, we used a fixed index annuity with a GLWB rider, giving them more control over the future of their contract.

In addition, for each year that Robert and Cheryl deferred taking income from the annuity, their guaranteed income payouts increased. For some who are unsure of an exact retirement date but are looking for something to fall back on if they decide to quit working tomorrow, fixed index annuities with income riders can be a solid option.

Robert and Cheryl said it changed the way they lived and worked. They realized they weren't at the mercy of the market and, regardless of when they decided they were fed up with working, they knew they would be able to retire. This gave them the ability to enter "Job Optional" status, knowing they could retire at any time. Still, for some, even the upside potential offered in a fixed index annuity—with rider options—just isn't enough.

Variable Annuities

Variable annuities[16] have declined in popularity due to a high degree of negative publicity attributable to excessive fees found therein. As I mentioned previously in my discussion on efficiency, variable annuities have often been peddled as a so-called silver bullet for retirement. Financial professionals sell these products because of their upside potential and auxiliary guarantees, but it's important to remember that they all come at a serious cost. When making a deposit into a variable annuity, the first thing to understand is you are purchasing a "security." Far from the usual associations with the word security, when we talk about security products in finance, we're talking about products that can lose value. Fixed and fixed index annuities are not classified as securities because you cannot lose your original principal due to market fluctuations.

Variable annuities essentially invest your money in mutual funds or exchange-traded funds until you begin taking income. At the time you turn on income, your income is calculated based on the performance of the mutual funds or exchange-traded funds that underlie your investment. This gives you more upside potential, but also means you could lose money and suffer through retirement with an income based on an asset that took heavy losses in a market correction.

One attractive part of a variable annuity is the tax-deferral feature inherently found within all types of annuities. This allows your capital gains, dividends, and interest to be deferred until the withdrawal of the funds in the future, much like a **non-deductible IRA**. It may only benefit the wealthiest of Americans in the highest of tax brackets, though. The downside of annuities is your distributions are always taxed as ordinary income rather than the more preferential capital gain or dividend rates. This is where you must weigh the cost of variable annuities heavily.

A NON-DEDUCTIBLE IRA IS IN MANY WAYS THE SAME AS A TRADITIONAL IRA. THE CONTRIBUTION LIMITS ARE THE SAME, THE MONEY GROWS TAX-DEFERRED, AND TO BE ELIGIBLE TO CONTRIBUTE, YOU MUST HAVE RECEIVED EARNED INCOME. THE DIFFERENCE IS, WITH A NONDEDUCTIBLE IRA, YOU AREN'T ALLOWED TO DEDUCT YOUR CONTRIBUTION FROM YOUR INCOME TAXES LIKE YOU CAN WITH A TRADITIONAL IRA.

These products not only contain the costs and ongoing fees associated with the mutual funds, or exchange-traded funds in which your money is invested, but you also must pay a separate charge for the insurance product wrapper itself, most commonly known as a mortality and expense charge. These charges vary widely and are typically more than 1 percent per year. However, they can be significantly less.

I once had a high-income earning client in the highest marginal tax bracket with a substantial portion of his wealth in after-tax accounts generating significant taxable gains, which dramatically reduced his annual returns. We found a low-cost variable annuity offering low-cost exchange-traded funds as the investment options; the monthly costs of the account were only a flat twenty dollars per month. After projecting after-tax returns of traditional investments outside of the variable annuity in contrast to those within a variable annuity, it was more advantageous to pay the low cost for the tax-deferred wrapper.

I tell you this to demonstrate I don't definitively dislike variable annuities—each product can have its place at the table. (And it's important for you to keep an open mind and set aside your bias before beginning your retirement planning.) Unfortunately, this is not the way most variable annuities are sold or used. In my experience, this is one investment that is typically misunderstood by those who aren't well acquainted with financial services.

For example, I had a gentleman seek me out to have me give a second opinion on his retirement strategy, which had much of his life savings invested in a variable annuity with a death benefit rider. This was a few short years after the 2008 market collapse, and it had taken a huge bite out of the value of his account (the "real money"). He had recently uncovered the extent of the annual fees he was paying within this account—including a base mortality and expense charge of 1.25 percent, an average of one percent in expenses for the investment's underlying mutual fund, plus another .95 percent per year for a death benefit rider.

His "real money" was worth significantly less than his original deposit of $500,000: It had declined to roughly $400,000, but he said he couldn't get out of it as he would lose a substantial death benefit worth around $600,000. His annual fees added up to 3.2 percent, but because the death benefit fee was charged against the death benefit value, his actual costs added up to about $14,700 per year (or about 3.7 percent of his "real money").

Deposit : $500,000

Accumulation Value	Death Benefit Value
"Real $" $400,000	$600,000

This meant his mutual funds had to overcome an almost 4 percent annual hurdle to even credit any interest at all. In all likelihood, his $400,000 would never match the $600,000 death benefit, even over a lifetime. I asked a very basic question: "What is your death benefit on this account?" He responded, very obviously, that it was $600,000. The reality was, $400,000 of the death benefit was made up of his own money and the insurance company only had to pay out $200,000 out of their own pocket.

Now, $200,000 is nothing to sneeze at, but taxes had to be calculated into that, as well. Since it was in an IRA, it would be taxable at his beneficiaries' highest marginal tax bracket. If his beneficiaries paid an average 30 percent in taxes on the $200,000 lump sum, once federal, state and local taxes were factored in, the net death benefit to the heirs would only amount to $140,000 after taxes. The cost of this death benefit was .95 percent of $600,000, or $5,700.

Instead, we moved the funds out of the mutual fund wrapper, eliminating the 1.25 percent mortality and expense charges, in addition to the .95 percent death benefit fee. We were able to cut costs by over $10,000 per year, unleashing the true growth potential of the "real money." We also elected to use the $5,700 he had been paying in death benefit charges to purchase a $300,000 tax-free life insurance death benefit that could also be used while he was living to cover potential long-term care expenses.

NEVER FORGET, THERE IS NO SUCH THING AS A PERFECT INVESTMENT— IF IT LOOKS TOO GOOD TO BE TRUE, THEN IT PROBABLY IS.

These costs, along with the convoluted and often confusing nature of these products, make them the most hated investment vehicle on the market today. Financial writer, Jane Bryant Quinn, went so far as to say, "You rarely find me so deeply angry at a common investment product that I dream of blowing it to smithereens." I have yet to find anyone with a variable annuity who has come to visit our office and truly understood how their investment vehicle operated and what the costs really were.

Variable annuities have their place, but for most individuals, they are one of the worst investments you could make with your retirement savings—so exercise caution.

ANNUITY QUICK-LOOK

IMMEDIATE	FIXED	FIXED INDEX	FIXED INDEX WITH GLWB	VARIABLE
Guaranteed income for a set period or lifetime	Fixed rate of return for a set period	Principal protection with returns tied to a specified market-based index	Same as Fixed Index with added feature of guaranteed lifetime income	Market risk to principal with ability to add various riders for income or death benefit guarantees

When it comes to creating a guaranteed lifetime income strategy, you may want to evaluate various SPIA and GLWB options. This will be the only way to truly guarantee that you will never run out of income during retirement, regardless of market fluctuations. Any product comes at a cost, of course; with fixed and fixed index annuities, you can easily see you will be giving up the growth potential and flexibility that traditional market-based investment options offer. I tend to lean away from having too high a concentration of annuities, opting instead to do my income planning through strategies we will soon discuss, such as flooring, segmented income or flexible withdrawal strategies. However, I am often surprised by how many retirees are willing to concede upside potential and flexibility in exchange for greater certainty in retirement, exemplifying the uniqueness we all have when it comes to structuring the appropriate retirement income strategy.

MEET TERRY

Terry was retiring from BF Goodrich after years of working on the factory floor. When our Vice President, Marshal Johnson, and I first walked into our conference room and began reviewing Terry's current investments, his situation seemed pretty straightforward. Everything was saved in his 401(k) plan from work with very little after-tax savings available. Terry said he hadn't looked at his statements in years; he just plugged away, pouring monthly contributions into his plan along with a generous employer match.

He said the day before he came to visit us was the first time he had looked at his statements in years—he was dumfounded to realize he was a millionaire. There was a little over $1 million in his retirement plan from work and he wanted to retire in a few short years at the age of 62.

After reviewing various retirement income strategies, we found Terry could potentially double or triple the value of his accounts over his lifetime by using more of a market-based strategy with greater risk and still satisfy his retirement income needs. On the other side of the spectrum, we could use a strategy that focused on preserving his principal and guaranteeing him a lifetime of income.

Terry told us his heirs would be blown away if their dad even left behind a couple hundred thousand dollars, let alone $1 million or more. He went on to share with us that he never wanted to think about the stock market and didn't want to depend on the market doing even average to succeed. He never wanted to worry about the Dow dropping several hundred points in a day. He focused on the guaranteed options offered by annuity products, because his main concern was knowing he would have enough income to last the rest of his life.

The last time Terry came in to visit with us, he mentioned his children wanted to know what we discussed. Terry went on to share that his children have always known him as a bit of a tight wad, but now, when there's something he wants to do, he does it! He no longer frets about the market or if he has enough. Instead, he spends his time focused on what he enjoys. Terry spends his time with grandkids and tinkering with old cars. He even purchased an old Firebird he had his eye on for years, just like when he was a kid. Terry was able to spend with confidence because he had a Purpose Based Retirement strategy built just for him.

Many individuals we work with aren't willing to give up as much flexibility as Terry was and are often seeking to leave behind as much as possible in the way of a legacy for the next generation. In that respect, you may want to evaluate some of the following alternatives for your very own retirement income strategy.

Flooring

Flooring is a variation of a traditional guaranteed lifetime income strategy that offers more flexibility and upside potential, simply with less guarantees. To begin the planning process with this strategy, you will need to identify and separate your pay checks from your play checks during retirement. In other words, what expenses will you have during retirement that you simply cannot live without, and which would you be able to give up, either periodically or all together in a worst-case scenario?

At the beginning of retirement, you may recognize that those three months a year to spend in a warmer climate or the annual vacation you plan to take your grandkids on is not a need. But, when push comes to shove, you spent your whole life saving to be able to do these things, and you're going to do them whether it puts your retirement income strategy in jeopardy or not.

There are those, however, who have enough inherent financial discipline to follow a flooring strategy, guaranteeing the income they cannot live without and utilizing at-risk income strategies to supplement for your "play checks," such as interest, dividend and/or even bond laddering strategies.

Dr. Pfau had this to say regarding using annuities as a flooring strategy: "If you have a certain amount of expenses per year, say $80,000 or whatever the case may be, we'll first look at things like Social Security which is a guaranteed lifetime income, if you have any other pension, that sort of thing. And then if there's still a gap, rather than trying to manage your whole retirement through these distributions from an investment portfolio, look at using income guarantees, an annuity offering lifetime income protection. This can help manage the longevity risk of not knowing how long you're going to live and help manage that sequence of returns risk, where having to take distributions from a declining portfolio balance becomes increasingly risky in retirement. Basing that more on insurance as the first building block."[17]

MEET BILL AND BROOKE

Bill and Brooke fit the bill perfectly. With substantial pre-tax and after-tax savings (more than enough to handle their retirement income needs), they decided to structure a guaranteed lifetime income strategy with their pre-tax retirement savings. Then, they structured a portion of their after-tax savings to generate dividend income from equities. The income they expected from the equities was income they didn't think they necessarily needed—they had Social Security, pensions and their annuities, after all—but Bill and Brooke wanted the flexibility to know they could get a couple thousand extra dollars a month if they decided to live an extravagant year from time to time or gift more money to their children.

For them, flooring provided the security they needed and the flexibility they desired. Most recently, they wanted to take their grandkids on a Disney cruise; all nine grandkids plus their eight parents! The flexibility this plan offered was perfect for their lifestyle, and the flooring gave them the confidence they needed to do those little extra things every so often. For others desiring more growth potential and flexibility than a flooring strategy offers, it may be worth evaluating a segmented income strategy with varying degrees of risk.

Segmented Income

One of my personal favorite income strategies is a segmented income strategy, which provides for significant upside over the years while offering the psychological protection most retirees need to succeed. Retirement income strategies often fail because retirees panic during a down market. Why? Because everything was stuffed into an investment portfolio without specifically identifying which pieces of the portfolio would be spent down first. As a result, when the market tanks, retirees liquidate investments without discrimination and may never recover.

A segmented income strategy addresses the problem of immediate market volatility and gives a sort of buffer to buy themselves time to continue to invest funds needed to replace their first leg of income at some point in the future (typically 5-15 years).

Once we have identified the income someone needs from the investment portfolio, we begin by segmenting off portions of the portfolio to be spent at different stages over the course of retirement. These are usually split into two to four different segments, depending on the amount of time a person expects to spend in retirement. The segments include a variety of investments or insurance products offering varying degrees of security and potential.

The first leg of income needs will be structured to satisfy five to 15 years' worth of retirement income needs, dependent on products available and the client's desire for income security. This first leg of income could be generated using an annuity, conservative investment portfolio or bond ladder—it's important that the first leg of income be conservatively allocated.

Essentially, we are creating an anti-anxiety pill for retirement, to allow your other investments to endure the market's ups and downs just as you did during your working years without causing panic. I heard many retirees over the years say they need to get out of the market because they can't take the risk anymore. "Why?" I ask. They always say it's because they don't have the time they previously had to make up the losses.

What they aren't realizing is that they still have a significant investment life left that may last another twenty to thirty years or more. The difference is that you now have monthly income needs you didn't have during your working years. Segmented income strategies can be helpful because they can buy you time to continue investing the funds you don't immediately need in more aggressive investments or allocations for long term growth. This allows our second and third legs of income needs to take on greater risk and potential for growth. If a major market downturn occurs, you know your immediate income needs are taken care of for a period on the funds that either suffered no or minor losses. The second and third legs of income have suffered losses to increasing degrees but have time to recover.

Your second leg of income assets may be structured in a more moderate allocation to be used five to 15 years down the road, while your third leg may be structured in a more aggressive allocation for

10 to 20 years down the road or more. I like to say we are making you young again.

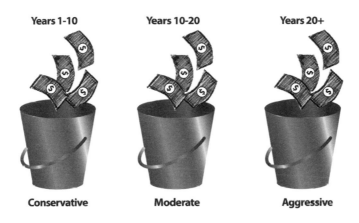

Years 1-10	Years 10-20	Years 20+
Conservative	Moderate	Aggressive

MEET RORY AND TINA

I once worked with a couple, Rory and Tina, who leaned toward the segmented strategy for their retirement years. When they retired at 62 and filed for early Social Security income, they had a gap to fill, since they didn't have a pension benefit from their employer.

We used an annuity, guaranteed to satisfy the first 10 years of their retirement income needs. Then, we set aside additional funds to be invested in a moderate risk investment portfolio of exchange-traded funds and individual stocks to be left alone to grow for the next ten years. After that, Rory and Tina would use those funds to satisfy the following 10 years of income needs.

As a result, we had satisfied 20 years of retirement income needs, taking them into their early 80s. Due to potential longevity, Rory and Tina wanted to plan on needing income into their early-to-mid-90s, so we established a third leg of income in a more aggressive investment portfolio to be left alone for the next 20 years or more.

If you think about it, Rory and Tina were investing as if they were 62 on their first leg of income needs, 52 on their second leg of income needs and 42 on their third leg of income needs. They were now able to wrap their heads around taking risk with their retirement funds, knowing the funds they don't need for a decade could dip 10 or 20 percent in a major market downturn and the funds they won't need for 20 years may lose 20 or 30 percent, but also that they had bought themselves the time to make up the losses.

A strategy such as this is not meant to be static. Over time, we will need to rebalance the accounts as we spend down the first leg of income and experience growth in the second and third legs. The funds from our more aggressive investments will need to be shifted to a more conservative position to be more protective of our gains over time. Another interesting strategy is known as a flexible withdrawal strategy, which we will cover next.

Flexible Withdrawal Strategy

A **flexible withdrawal strategy** is just that, it's flexible!

It may require a more hands-on approach than some of the more set-it-and-forget-it strategies discussed previously. Nevertheless, it might also offer significantly more growth potential as well.

Within a flexible withdrawal strategy, we will structure a portfolio with a variety of different investments offering enough diversification for us to know there will always be a place for us to go—even in a down market—to generate income without violating the cardinal rule of investments ("buy low and sell high"). One of the biggest risks for retirees is the chance that they may suffer a significant loss and be forced to sell depressed assets in a poor market, but a flexible withdrawal strategy can address this by holding a significant number of uncorrelated investments. That way, if a market downturn affects one side of the portfolio, the noncorrelated assets from the other side of the portfolio can supply your income.

> A FLEXIBLE WITHDRAWAL STRATEGY IS A SYSTEMATIC WITHDRAWAL THAT ALLOWS A SHAREHOLDER TO WITHDRAW MONEY FROM AN EXISTING MUTUAL FUND PORTFOLIO; A FIXED OR VARIABLE AMOUNT IS WITHDRAWN AT REGULAR INTERVALS.

MEET MARC AND JOLEEN

I met with a realtor and administrative assistant, Marc and Joleen, who were a few years from retirement. They wanted to implement a retirement strategy that took fewer risks than what they were taking in their portfolio during their working years.

We split funds across various equity and bond portfolios in addition to using a fixed index annuity that earned interest credits based on the S&P 500. Traditionally, a flexible strategy might use bonds, preferred stocks, and real estate investments as your "safe" fixed income alternative instead of the fixed index annuity. Research shows with the right fixed index annuity, though, you can experience greater growth at a significantly lower risk.[18]

Below Median and Above Median Bond Return Environments (1927-2016)

	Bellow Median Bond Return Enviroments Average Return	Above Median Bond Return Enviroments Average Return	Overall Period Average Return
Long Term Gov't Bonds	1.87%	9.00%	5.43%
Large Cap Stocks	11.43%	9.84%	10.63%
FIA	4.42%	7.55%	5.98%
60/40 (Stocks & Bonds)	7.60%	9.50%	8.55%
60/20/20 (Stocks, Bonds & FIA)	8.12%	9.21%	8.66%
60/40 (Bonds & FIA)	8.63%	8.92%	8.77%

Source: 2017 SBBI Yearbook, Roger G. Ibbotson, Duff & Phelps; Zebra Capital; AnnGen Development, LLC

Professor Roger Ibbotson illustrates in his whitepaper (referenced in the above chart) the diversification benefits of utilizing a fixed index annuity in conjunction with other asset classes to reduce volatility and risk in a rising interest rate environment while maintaining growth potential."

In a low-interest rate environment, allocating more funds to traditional fixed income investments has meant taking on unnecessary interest rate risks if interest rates begin to rise. Think of it this way:

say you buy a bond today, paying 3 percent interest, but next year the same bond might pay 4 percent. If you must sell your 3 percent bond that year, you'll have to sell it at a discount because of the more attractive, higher interest-paying bonds available.

In addition to interest rate risks, bonds face default risks—even the highest quality bonds can default; at one time, the Lehman Brothers bonds were rated very highly. By using a fixed index annuity that credits your contract based on 75 percent of the S&P 500's gains, gains are locked in every two years and protect your principal. In short, you can avoid the default and interest rate risk of traditional fixed income investments. Also, there's the possibility of achieving a higher rate of return due to the historical returns of the stock market versus fixed income products. This isn't to say that fixed income or bonds are obsolete, but you may want to investigate diversifying with these types of fixed income alternatives. After all, the age-old rule of diversification cannot be overlooked.

The point here with the flexible withdrawal strategy is that we generate income from whichever investments perform the best, locking in our gains periodically as we take withdrawals. But, if those investments experienced losses, we would be able to shift withdrawals to those defensive tools that were either performing well during market downturns or experiencing little to no loss. Such defensive tools include bonds, commodities (gold) or even guaranteed products (fixed index annuities).

This strategy offers significantly more upside potential and flexibility than the other strategies discussed previously. However, there are no guarantees of annual returns or performance because all investments have some degree of market risk. Now, instead of a fixed index annuity, we could have utilized a fixed annuity. It offers more predictability, but this strategy will always carry an inherent risk due to the exposure created through the use of various at-risk investments.

Marc and Joleen eventually inherited funds from a previous generation and had goals of not only preserving, but also growing those funds to leave behind for their children. They were more driven by what they may leave behind than the income security they would have during their own retirement years. They didn't mind some market risk but wanted a place they could go for income while the market recovered after an inevitable future pullback. Not long ago, they were on vacation with friends in Hawaii for a couple weeks. Meanwhile, there was a nearly 10 percent market correction, with the news headlines shouting doom and gloom. They mentioned that while the group of them was gathered around the TV, their friends were in a panic. One couple even called their advisor to liquidate their investment accounts. All the while, Marc and Joleen said they had to keep their happiness to themselves, as they knew they were OK no matter what—all thanks to the foresight they had in preparing for the worst.

In the end, as I hope you can see, your retirement income strategy is of personal preference. They all have their own pros and cons.

Independence

One more thing to keep in mind as you are evaluating various retirement income strategies and the products therein should be your advisor's access to tools. Not all financial professionals have the same licensing, and even among those who do, the range of companies they work with greatly affects their ability to access the right tools for the job.

Many soon-to-be-retirees switch financial advisors as they prepare for the next stage of their lives (or, for some, they seek a financial advisor for the first time). Inevitably, as they search for the right financial professional, they find certain advisors avoid some of the strategies altogether, which is likely because of licensing or employment restrictions.

For instance, when it comes to annuities, there are hundreds of options. In the same sense, there are numerous products and product types in the stock or bond market, and the quality of these products can vary widely due to rates or the strength of the carrier offering the product.

I had a couple once visit to get a second opinion on the financial tools they had been sold a couple of years earlier. They were working with a major national firm with offices across the country. This firm, however, focused its insurance offerings largely on the proprietary products they offered.

The couple purchased a fixed annuity paying 2.5 percent per year with a 10-year surrender charge period and no guarantees that the interest crediting rate wouldn't decrease. Had they worked with an independent advisor with the ability to shop amongst carriers, circumstances might have been different. They might have arranged for a 3.5 percent fixed rate annuity with a five-year surrender charge period and a guarantee the rate would never change.

You may also see the same with fixed index annuities. One company may offer a 20 percent participation rate in the S&P 500, while another highly rated carrier offers 50 percent or more.

One thing to keep in mind is the "financial planning" world (really the brokerage world) was founded on securities offerings, such as stocks, bonds, mutual funds, variable annuities, etc., which large national financial firms often developed in-house and sold to their clients. Today, very few national financial firms are selling proprietary products, but they almost exclusively still focus on at-risk investment offerings. At the same time, they ignore, and poo-poo fixed and fixed index annuities altogether because of the enormous amount of income that has been generated through their investment partners over the years.

We are beginning to see a shift in the industry, where more national firms are offering products with better guarantees. However, their range of options are always limited due to the agreements they have with their product partners. For instance, say an advisor is with Big Box Megabrokerage firm. Big Box Megabrokerage might have what is called a revenue-sharing agreement with the Lifetime Moneycorp Inc. company. When Big Box Megabrokerage's advisors sell a Lifetime Moneycorp Inc. product, Lifetime Moneycorp shares a portion of that revenue back to Big Box Megabrokerage, and sometimes to the advisor—something commonly known as a "kickback."

The reason for this is obvious: Lifetime Moneycorp wants to incentivize agents to sell its product. Who do you think ultimately pays for that kickback? That's right, whoever is buying the product. And whoever is buying could pay twice, in a certain sense. Not only are they subsidizing the revenue-sharing system up front with their purchase, they are also at risk of opportunity costs if their agent passed over better products to sell the Lifetime Moneycorp product (which was more lucrative to the agent).

As Dr. Pfau said in the "Retire with Purpose" podcast, "It's advisors who are just licensed on one side that I think increasingly recognize the value of both, and you are finding more advisors today who are more comfortable looking at both the insurance and the investment worlds to build a more holistic plan."

To get the best range of options, you will want to work with a truly independent advisor who is not tied to a national brokerage firm. This provides you access to shop the universe of options available.

Social Security Planning[19]

During your retirement income planning, don't overlook Social Security! Your retirement income strategy is made up of many puzzle pieces, and, for most Americans, their Social Security income will be a primary source of retirement income. Despite this, it is one that is often undervalued. Too often, this is because people make quick decisions regarding Social Security, overlooking strategies and costing themselves thousands and even hundreds of thousands of dollars. Let's look at the real value of your Social Security benefit so you see what I mean. If your benefit is $1,000 per month, it would take at least $300,000 in private assets to generate that kind of income over the course of retirement—which only allows you to withdraw 4 percent and doesn't factor in market volatility or the numerous tax advantages afforded to Social Security income. Now, you wouldn't

YOUR FULL RETIREMENT AGE

Year of Birth	Full Retirement Age
1937 or earlier	65
1938	65 and 2 months
1939	65 and 4 months
1940	65 and 6 months
1941	65 and 8 months
1942	65 and 10 months
1943-1954	66
1955	66 and 2 months
1956	66 and 4 months
1957	66 and 6 months
1958	66 and 8 months
1959	66 and 10 months
1960 or later	67

go out and blow $300,000 without doing your research, so why would you do so with your Social Security benefit?

Simply hitting retirement age and filing for your benefit without doing any research is akin to just that—it's irresponsible. Social Security filing and benefit options are regularly evolving, so whatever strategy you have today may need to change by the time you get to retirement. For instance, at one time, you could collect spousal benefits while your spouse was still delaying benefits. This allowed you to both file under your own income records later in life when deferral credits had fattened up their monthly checks.

In the Bipartisan Budget Act of 2015, which President Barack Obama signed into law, this "loophole" closed, but when it was popular, Social Security beneficiaries collected essentially extra benefits over and above typical filing strategies, often adding tens of thousands of extra dollars to a retiree's bottom line. There are unique circumstances for divorcees and widows as well that may or may not be closed in the future, and many times these benefits are overlooked.

The basic rules for Social Security are that the agency calculates your monthly benefit based off your income earnings during your career, your life expectancy, and what age you file relative to your full retirement age. Your full retirement age or FRA may be 66 to 67, depending on the year you were born. You can file for your benefits as early as 62 and have your monthly check reduced from what it would be at FRA. Or, you can delay filing to age 70, for which your monthly check will increase from what it would have been if you filed at FRA. Of course, even if you have a sizeable gap in your career—a common scenario for many whose careers were largely domestic or based on volunteering in their communities—you can file to receive spousal benefits, or up to fifty percent of what your spouse qualifies for at their FRA.

Yet, these are not universal rules. You may have special circumstances if your spouse died, or if you are caring for a minor or disabled child of a divorced or deceased spouse. It pays to poke around and be sure you know all the rules and exceptions that pertain to your unique situation.

For instance, a 60-year-old widow who was struggling to make ends meet after losing her husband hadn't realized that she was eligible to file for a survivor Social Security benefit. She learned about the special provisions that applied to her situation allowed her to file for benefits immediately. She may have missed out on a few months of benefits, but once she filed, the extra monthly income she received changed her life. Where she was once struggling to make ends meet, she was now able to do things she couldn't prior, like going out to eat with a group of longtime friends.

My mom was another case of a unique situation allowing for incredible Social Security planning opportunities. The Bipartisan Budget Act of 2015 may have eliminated special filing opportunities for married couples, but it left those same rules in place for divorcees, leading to some criticism of the government "subsidizing divorce." When Mom reached her full retirement age (FRA), she could file for spousal benefits based on my father's (her ex-husband's) Social Security record, to the tune of approximately $1,100 per month. Had she filed for her own benefits, she would have received roughly $1,200 per month. By deciding to first file on my father's benefit, though, she could delay her own benefit and earn delayed filing credits to age 70. Then, on reaching seventy, she could switch her filing to her own earnings record, giving her a $1,500 monthly check. That is a bigger check going into her pocket for the rest of her life.

MEET STEVE AND BARBARA

Steve and Barbara were retiring early from the same company at age sixty. Their company offered a variety of pension benefits. The most beneficial, after thorough analysis, was a 10-year, period-certain option guaranteeing all their income needs would be satisfied until age 70. This allowed for a few different planning opportunities. One opportunity, and the most obvious, was their ability to get the highest monthly Social Security check by delaying filing to age 70.

The second and less obvious opportunity was with their taxes. An often-overlooked feature of Social Security is that since 1983, a portion of many retirees' Social Security benefit is subject to federal income taxes. Due to Social Security originally being an untaxed benefit altogether, many people forget things have changed. Today, depending on your income sources and their taxability, up to 85 percent of your Social Security benefits can be taxed during retirement. With appropriate planning, however, you may be able to eliminate these taxes altogether, as Steve and Barbara did.

They retired with a substantial amount of pre-tax assets in their 401(k)s, which they would not require for retirement income needs. It essentially became an overblown emergency fund. Unfortunately, due to required minimum distributions on 401(k)s, Steve and Barbara came across an issue. After age 70 ½, they would be forced to begin taking taxable distributions from their traditional retirement accounts, regardless of whether they needed the income. Failing to take RMDs could result in a 50 percent tax penalty of whatever the missed RMD is. But, as we looked down the road, we saw that Steve and Barbara's RMDs would push most of their Social Security income into taxable range in addition to pushing them into higher marginal tax brackets.

Thankfully, since they had a decade before RMDs kicked in, they used this period to convert most of their tax-deferred retirement dollars to after-tax retirement accounts which will grow tax-free via Roth IRA conversions. Roth IRAs can grow tax-free without the requirement for distributions until the death of the owner. This almost eliminated the taxes Steve and Barbara would have paid on their Social Security benefits, and minimized the amount of federal, state and local taxes they would pay over their lifetime. It may even save them on Medicare premiums over their lifetime. When it comes to Social Security planning, the rules are always changing. As you can see from the previous examples, though, there are many potential landmines, and many opportunities to avoid them if you plan. If you view your retirement as a puzzle, you should see that Social Security is one very large piece!

Tax Planning

Another piece of your retirement puzzle that is often overlooked? The benefits of tax planning opportunities, particularly within your retirement income strategy. Too often this is reduced to a single question: Which bucket of funds should you spend first—the taxable, tax-deferred or tax-free?

This isn't necessarily as easy of a question as it may seem. Many textbooks recommend you spend the taxable dollars first to preserve the tax benefits of the tax-deferred and tax-free dollars. However, this should not be generalized, as everyone is unique in this respect. There are more factors that we must consider before deciding how to approach assets with different tax situations.

Our team worked with a couple who was lucky enough to diversify their tax dollars in such a way that they had substantial funds in each of these buckets. This allowed for planning opportunities many don't have when everything is in one bucket. Most often, retirees are highly concentrated in the tax-deferred bucket.

After projecting taxability both today and in the future—including potential penalties and taxation on Medicare and Social Security benefits—it made sense to use a blended withdrawal strategy, primarily aimed at minimizing their current and future tax obligations. We allocated the taxable dollars to their emergency fund, which we positioned to grow tax-deferred should they need the funds in the future. In the event emergency never arises, the asset will pass tax-free to their heirs. We then took a blended income from their tax-deferred IRAs and tax-free Roth IRAs, as well as cash value life insurance policies. This permitted us to level out RMDs over their lifetime, as well as minimize tax consequences today.

Retirement income planning isn't as simple as just throwing investments into a few accounts, setting up a regular distribution, and hoping things work out. There is much more involved than that if you want to have the confidence to spend during your retirement years.

For more on this topic, check out the Educational Videos section of the Howard Bailey website and watch our video, "Using Tax Buckets in a Retirement Strategy:"

https://howardbailey.com/educational-videos/tax-buckets/

CHAPTER 4: TAKEAWAYS, ACTIONS, AND NOTES

What are your biggest takeaways from this chapter?

_____

_____

_____

What are 3 action steps that you should work on now?

1. _____

2. _____

3. _____

What are 3 action steps for later?

1. _____

2. _____

3. _____

Notes:

_____

_____

_____

_____

_____

_____

CHAPTER FIVE

GROWTH PLANNING

I often say retirement is about income, not growth. Most of your life has been about growth—accumulation at all costs!—but in retirement, your focus must shift to income and making those funds last a lifetime. I reiterate these words regularly because today's retiree has been focused on nothing but growth their entire life. Turning those hard-earned assets into a regular income takes a major mental shift that most retirees struggle with.

I'm not saying you should ignore long-term growth during retirement. Many retirees will still be investing for the long-term when they first retire. It ultimately comes down to prioritization; in retirement, your priorities shouldn't focus on growth, your priorities shouldn't focus on the returns on your money, your priority should be the return of your money—cash flow.

However, once you have satisfied your cash flow needs using one of the previous strategies, then you can begin structuring some of your remaining assets for long-term

> "The seeds of an investment crisis have been sown. The only way to avoid a catastrophe is for plan participants, professionals, and regulators to shift the mind-set and metrics from asset value to income."
>
> ~Harvard Business Review, *The Crisis in Retirement Planning*[20]

growth which will be needed to play defense against inflation eroding your spending power.

Planning is about controlling what we can and playing defense against the rest. Your emergency fund should be priority No. 1, followed by a reliable income strategy that lends you the confidence needed to spend during retirement, and the long-term growth of the funds you may need down the road. Inflation will affect everyone differently. Your assets must take this into account and be adjusted accordingly when you might expect to spend them in retirement.

MEET LEE

Lee first walked into my office in 2010. Upon entering the conference room, I didn't even get a chance to sit down before he shared with me the outstanding job he had done saving for retirement. He said, "I'm 52 years old and have $740,000 saved for retirement." He shared with me that he had worked at the local gas company his entire career—I had guessed that much, since he sported a shirt with their logo and wears the same work shirt every time he comes in for his quarterly reviews. Lee had been working as much overtime as he possibly could to maximize his 401(k) contributions year after year. He was already debt-free and headed to an early retirement with a goal of retiring at 59 ½—a date he set because it was the earliest he thought he could access funds from his retirement account without a 10 percent tax penalty. He told me he didn't save his money so that he could leave it behind; quite the contrary. He wanted to retire early and spend as much as possible every month; straight to the point of handing over his last dollar and writing a bad check right before they put a nail in the coffin.

Lee didn't have any children or spouse to take over his lifelong savings. He wanted to enjoy his retirement to the fullest and do things he was never able to do while sacrificing time during his employment. Of course, **longevity risk** was a real concern for him. In addition, how would we know how much he could spend month in and month out without being able to predict market activity? In this case, a guaranteed income strategy was perfect. It provided Lee with a guaranteed income he could not outlive on a portion of his life savings, while leaving the rest for long-term inflation protection. Inflation was a real concern of his; he had longevity in his blood and had a significant chance that he could actually be retired longer than he worked!

> **LONGEVITY RISK IS THE RISK THAT THE AMOUNT OF MONEY AN INDIVIDUAL SAVES FOR RETIREMENT MIGHT NOT BE ENOUGH TO SUSTAIN THEM, DUE TO INCREASED LIFE EXPECTANCY.**

At Howard Bailey, we recommend setting aside a certain percent of a portfolio purely for inflation protection based on many factors that vary from person to person. In the case of Lee, we decided to set 40 percent of the assets in his income strategy to the side for long-term growth and inflation. We separated his assets to focus on two competing purposes: return of his money or income and return on his money or growth. Since Lee had about $740,000 in total assets to work with, we allotted about $400,000 to income-generating assets with the aim of generating $20,000 a year and put about $160,000 aside for future inflation protection. This left us with $140,000 to set aside for other potential needs and liabilities, such as health care expenses, and $40,000 for liquidity or emergency purposes.

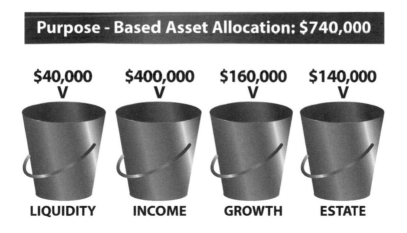

Purpose - Based Asset Allocation: $740,000

$40,000	$400,000	$160,000	$140,000
V	V	V	V
LIQUIDITY	INCOME	GROWTH	ESTATE

The amount anyone sets aside for both income and inflation protection will be determined by several different assumptions that each client and advisor will need to discuss. The numbers listed in Lee's example are general guidelines based on historical market returns and inflation growth.

As a result, these buckets could be nearly depleted over the course of retirement, allowing for annual inflation increases along the way, but since we implemented a guaranteed lifetime income strategy he would never run out of income even if he depleted 100 percent of his assets. These numbers are not precise because interest, inflation rate estimates and market considerations are at best assumptions, and also because spending habits of a retiree will change over time.

My college finance professor referred to these years as the "Go-Go," "Slow-Go" and "No-Go" years—meaning most retirees will see a reduction in discretionary spending over the span of their retirement, while they will also see an increase in spending on such things as health care. For instance, you may not be traveling, driving or golfing as much as you used to. You may also downsize and potentially even possess one car instead of two.

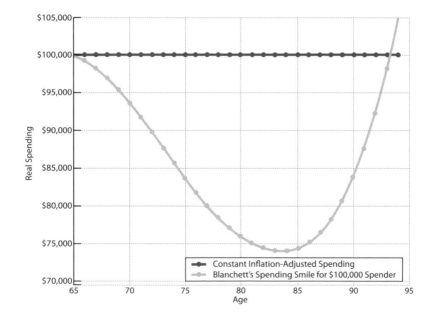

The research backs this up, showing the average retiree will see a reduction in expenses over their retirement careers that almost matches the historical rate of inflation, even when factoring in future health care expenses, which inflate at a higher rate compared to other sectors[21]. Furthermore, retirees with higher retirement expenses at the onset of retirement will be affected even less than those retirees with less retirement expenses at the onset of retirement. This is because retirees with higher expenses at the beginning of retirement typically have a larger budget for discretionary spending than those of retirees with lower expenses.

MEET MERLIN AND MARY

Merlin and Mary retired with a portfolio of over ten million dollars. They currently spend more than twenty thousand dollars a month. Their expenses are drastically different than most retirees. They spend six to eight months a year taking extravagant vacations. They maintain multiple homes across the country. They own several cars in addition to their daily drivers. They dine at high-end restaurants several times a week and sometimes pick up the tab for taking out their extended family. They have expensive extracurricular sporting activities they are regularly involved in.

In the future, as age takes its toll, Merlin and Mary won't be able to travel as extensively. They won't have any reason to have more than one or two homes or own cars beyond a daily driver. Their appetites will shrink, and they will likely not be physically able to participate in many of the sporting activities they enjoy today. They will most likely not feel the long-term effects of inflation, as their retirement expenses will easily be cut in half over the course of their first twenty or so years in retirement.

On the other end of the spectrum, and for many of the clients we work with, there is a couple who are conservative spenders, which got them to where they are in the first place. They saved a few million dollars for retirement and are stepping away from work in their 60s with more than enough saved. Frankly, even though they had great jobs earning great incomes, this couple realized they were no longer working for themselves, but instead were adding to the sum they would likely leave their beneficiaries, so they decided to retire. Their monthly expenses were just over $1,500 per month. They rarely dine out, live in a modest home, drive to all their vacation destinations, and own two used cars they hope to never have to replace.

This couple will feel the effects of inflation more because they have little in the way of discretionary expenses. They will have many of the same expenses in the future as they do today and will potentially face significant increases in health care spending. For this second couple, the focus isn't as much on income. It is about planning around inflation and putting an estate plan in place to insulate their legacy from major health care expenses and taxes.

Regardless of your spending habits, inflation is an unpredictable beast. Today, we may be able to point to research that states you will most likely not feel the effects of inflation. I may be able to point out that I have never seen a client need more income 10 years into retirement than they needed at the onset, but tomorrow may be a different story. We should always be playing defense against major risks such as this, even if we don't believe they will ever occur. Much like planning for potential long-term care expenses you may feel will never affect you, the future is truly unpredictable. So, let's plan with purpose instead of hope.

Finding the Right Inflation Hedge

Once you have determined the appropriate size of your inflation fund, it's time to find appropriate investments. You typically want to avoid conservative fixed-income products as inflation hedges. They will most likely pay a rate of return at or below the rate of inflation. Instead, you want your inflation hedge to grow faster than inflation and be compromised of diversified investments.

Despite what you may have heard on the latest radio or television advertisements, gold hasn't always been the best inflation hedge— particularly in the hyperinflation era of the late '70s and early '80s, gold inflated in tandem with overall inflation[22]. The same is true for dividend-paying stocks. The truth is, there are too many variables over too much time for us to define one specific inflation hedge that will perform the same forever.

Inflation doesn't affect you overnight. Tomorrow you will likely pay the same amount for the gallon of milk or carton of eggs at the store as you did today. Yet, inflation will eventually start to work against you, especially if your expenses are mostly non-discretionary. That gallon of eggs and carton of milk may cost the same tomorrow, but what about in a year? Five years? Ten? This is another reason you will be taking the most amount of risk with your inflation-hedging assets; these funds have time to go through the various ups and downs of at-risk markets that your other funds cannot afford, as you may need them for emergencies, income or healthcare costs.

The obvious result of inflation is having to pay more to fill the gas tank, buy a gallon of milk or even get a haircut—overall, an increase in your general cost of living. Inflation can become a real concern, which is why President Ronald Reagan said, "Inflation is as violent as a mugger, as frightening as an armed robber, and as deadly as a hit man."

The simplest form of inflation protection is finding ways to profit from the increasing prices of goods and services. The argument goes, stocks are claims on real assets, such as land, plants and equipment, which appreciate in value as overall prices increase. This fact is historically supported in general; over thirty-year periods, stock returns have been virtually unaffected by the inflation rate. This isn't always the case over shorter periods of time. Stocks have done historically well against inflation when the inflation rate is in the two to five percent range but have faltered when inflation has exceeded 5 percent.

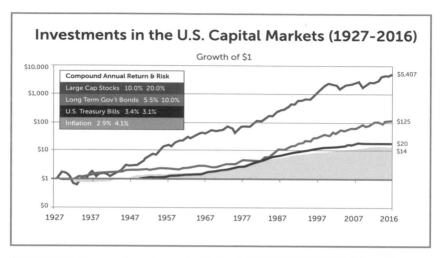

Investments in the U.S. Capital Markets (1927-2016)

Growth of $1

Compound Annual Return & Risk		
Large Cap Stocks	10.0%	20.0%
Long Term Gov't Bonds	5.5%	10.0%
U.S. Treasury Bills	3.4%	3.1%
Inflation	2.9%	4.1%

Source: https://www.dmi.com/wp-content/uploads/2018/10/ANX21230_Zebra_Ibbotson_
FIA_Whitepaper.pdf

So, while stocks can provide great long-term inflation protection, you may want to also diversify into alternative investments to ensure proper inflation protection, especially if we see periods of hyperinflation. When it comes to your assets that are aimed at protecting against inflation, you will want to avoid the bond market. The exception is for **Treasury Inflation Protection Securities (TIPS)**, which are Treasury bonds whose principal value increases with inflation and decreases with deflation and returns the adjusted principal or original principal (which ever is greater) to the investor upon maturity. This is one of the most conservative inflation-hedging options available to your portfolio.

> TREASURY INFLATION PROTECTED SECURITIES (TIPS) REFER TO A TREASURY SECURITY THAT IS INDEXED TO INFLATION IN ORDER TO PROTECT INVESTORS FROM THE NEGATIVE EFFECTS OF INFLATION.

Gold and other commodities also perform well in periods of high and increasing inflation, but long-term the results have not been so spectacular. For instance, gold has only returned a little less than one percentage point per year over that of the inflation rate in the past few centuries. That doesn't mean commodities don't have a place as an inflation hedge; you just might want to include investments in companies that will profit from increases in commodity prices, such as miners, drillers, storage facilities and transporters of commodities. Real estate exposure can be another effective inflation hedge as part of a diversified portfolio.

To round out your long-term growth portfolio for inflation protection, you should consider investing internationally. If inflation were to skyrocket, we would most certainly see a fall in the value of the dollar — in this case, foreign investments would act as an automatic inflation hedge.

Roth Conversion Opportunities

By segmenting our portfolios with different risk levels and asset types, we usually find ourselves presented with more tax planning opportunities than if all investments are in the same proverbial pot.

One tax crunch many retirees find themselves in is with their IRA and 401(k) assets. As I've discussed previously regarding RMDs, even if you don't need income from your traditional IRA, you may find yourself in a tricky tax scenario. Remember, traditional IRAs are tax-deferred, not tax-free. One way to avoid potentially being pushed into a higher tax bracket in later retirement is to pay taxes on those IRA assets now, and then allow them to grow tax-free in a **Roth IRA**.

First, let's unpack the basic difference between traditional and Roth IRAs. One of the ways I like to describe the difference is by using a common complaint I hear at family gatherings. Many in my extended family are farmers, and

A ROTH IRA IS AN INDIVIDUAL RETIREMENT PLAN THAT BEARS MANY SIMILARITIES TO THE TRADITIONAL IRA. THE BIGGEST DISTINCTION BETWEEN THE TWO IS HOW THEY'RE TAXED. ROTH IRAS ARE FUNDED WITH AFTER-TAX DOLLARS; THE CONTRIBUTIONS ARE NOT TAX DEDUCTIBLE. BUT WHEN YOU START WITHDRAWING FUNDS, QUALIFIED DISTRIBUTIONS ARE TAX FREE.

they have a lot of experience with working hard, only to see the fruits of their labors diminished by weather, insects, disease, foraging animals and—taxes. A common lament is wishing they could pay taxes on their seed, then grow their crops and sell the harvest tax-free. This is really the difference between a traditional IRA and a Roth IRA.

With a traditional IRA, you get a deduction for the taxes you would normally pay today, and it grows tax-deferred—until you start withdrawing money from your IRA. Then, you will pay a full income tax on your original contributions and any gains you made over the last several decades of investing.

Just to make sure he gets his cut, Uncle Sam has a rule that, after you turn seventy-and-one-half, you must withdraw at least a certain percentage (based on your life expectancy) of your account every year. These are the RMDs we discussed prior, the required withdrawals that can force you to not just pay more in federal, state and local taxes, but also on your Social Security benefits (and potentially even higher Medicare premiums).

By contrast, with a Roth IRA you pay income taxes on the money that goes into the account. You won't pay taxes on the funds you withdraw, which means that both your contributions and any gains they have made will come out of the account tax-free. The money that has already been taxed won't have required minimum distributions. If there is money left in the account when you die, your heirs must take RMDs, but those RMDs will still be tax free.

Few people would choose to convert their traditional IRA to a Roth as a lump sum. Can you imagine the tax consequences of paying income taxes on hundreds and thousands of dollars all at once? Converting smaller portions (just enough to fill up your current tax bracket) over a decade or so can greatly decrease the impact of traditional IRA RMDs on your taxable situation.

One opportunity to convert funds may be during a dip in the market. While your IRA assets are negatively affected, it might make sense to convert the depressed assets from your traditional IRA to a Roth IRA. You will pay less in ordinary income taxes today while the value is depressed, and then will be able to take advantage of having a larger tax-free value when the market rebounds. This takes your new Roth funds to higher heights.

Another unique opportunity has presented itself in the Tax Cuts and Jobs Act of 2017 (TCJA). After Congress passed the TCJA, Roth conversions essentially went on sale. We previously recommended you make Roth conversions in the 15 percent brackets and below, while also doing the same in the 25 percent bracket if you have substantial tax-deferred retirement accounts and/or taxable income in retirement.

The TCJA shifted the goal line, though; those who were in the 15 percent bracket are now in a 12 percent bracket, the 25 percent bracket is now the 22 percent bracket and the 24 percent bracket covers married couples filing jointly all the way up to $315,000 in taxable income. This means that, to fill up your bracket with money for a partial Roth conversion, you may have a lot more latitude to convert funds than what you would have in previous years. Keep in mind, though, these income tax brackets may only last until 2026, when the rules will "sunset" back to inflation-adjusted 2017 levels.

The chart on the next page shows a side-by-side comparison of how the 2017 marginal tax rates for single and married filers compare to the rates and income limits of the 2018 rates. Keep in mind, it's not just the monetary limits that are changed (albeit temporarily), but the actual percentage rates, as well.

You might think your CPA or tax preparer should be all over this opportunity, but you could be wrong.

MERGING INCOME TAX BRACKETS

2017			2018		
Rate	Single Filers	Married Filing Jointly	Rate	Single Filers	Married Filing Jointly
10%	$0 - $9,325	$0 - $18,650	10%	$0 - $9,525	$0 - $19,050
15%	$9,326 - $37,950	$18,651 - $75,900	12%	$9,525 - $38,700	$19,050 - $77,400
25%	$37,951 - $91,900	$75,901 - $153,100	22%	$38,700 - $82,500	$77,400 - $165,000
28%	$91,901 - $191,650	$153,101 - $233,350	24%	$82,500 - $157,500	$165,000 - $315,000
33%	$190,651 - $416,700	$233,351 - $416,700	32%	$157,500 - $200,000	$315,500 - $400,000
35%	$416,701-$418,400	$416,701-$470,700	35%	$200,000-$500,000	$400,000-$600,000
39.6%	$418,400	$470,700+	37%	$500,000+	$600,000+

Source: https://www.kdpllp.com/2017-vs-2018-federal-income-tax-brackets/

MEET MICHAEL AND PAULA

I once had a CPA, Michael, who came in to visit with our team for a second set of eyes on his personal investments. He was a fairly successful entrepreneur—he started, grew and ultimately sold his accounting practice at a relatively young age. After selling his practice in his early fifties, he decided to retire.

His wife, Paula, was still working part-time and together, they had minimal expenses due to becoming debt-free during Michael's working career. Essentially, they could live off her income. Paula enjoyed her job and didn't mind bridging the gap they had until they qualified to receive Social Security, at which point they planned to file early and live a comfortable retirement almost exclusively off their Social Security paychecks. He enjoyed managing his own investments and did a pretty decent job.

While the accounts were invested quite aggressively with little diversification, it was OK. They didn't ever plan to spend the funds and were holding a substantial emergency fund just in case. In addition, they kept their investing expenses low, using low-cost index funds. Many retirees don't want to have to worry about their money or think about day-to-day movements of the stock market ticker— Michael was an exception. He saw it as an exciting opportunity and shared with me that he spent an hour or two every day evaluating each of his holdings and studying the markets. It was fun for him.

When we asked to see a tax return, he seemed bewildered, saying he obviously had that under control. He was trained in tax planning, for goodness sakes. He went on to share with us that their tax bill was negligible, as their life savings was stuffed away in tax-deferred retirement accounts—largely his IRA from his working years. He was very proud of the fact that they maintained income in what was the 15 percent tax bracket at the time despite being technical millionaires. The reality was, he was doing what most CPAs do; looking back at the previous tax year and using their tax return as a scorecard to see how well they did. It's not the CPA's fault. It stems back to how they are trained and graded year after year by their clients. This is a viewpoint that is based on looking in the tiny, rearview mirror instead of the huge windshield in front of you; the taxes headed your way are the bugs splattering on it.

This CPA had accumulated over $1 million in retirement accounts and was less than 20 years away from being forced to take distributions out of them—when he didn't even need the money. As aggressively as he was investing, that million dollars could double twice over the next twenty years in a good market, turning into almost $4 million by the time they were 70 ½. Their RMDs would start at roughly $150,000 and only increase from there. This would take them from what is currently the 10 percent bracket all the way to the 25 percent bracket and beyond—their RMDs would likely get larger as their IRA grew and life expectancy shortened. It would force them to pay taxes on Social Security benefits that were previously tax-free when they first turned them on at 62 and potentially increase their

Medicare premiums, not to mention increase federal, state and local taxes each year.

After Michael redirected himself to look ahead, he and Paula structured a tax strategy that would keep them in a 15 percent tax bracket and potentially convert as much as half of their tax-deferred traditional retirement accounts to tax-free Roth accounts. With the lower and wider tax brackets created by the TCJA, they might even be able to convert all their tax-deferred savings into tax-free savings through converting larger amounts at lower rates, creating a truly tax-free retirement. Keep in mind, this tax sale is slated to last for a limited time. These rates are set to expire in 2025 and changes could happen sooner. This is one sale you don't want to let pass you by, or you'll be paying for it the rest of your life.

Watch Your Expenses

Another opportunity in the growth section of your portfolio is to minimize your ongoing fees and expenses—a simple way to put more growth on the table for long-term inflation protection. It is now easier than ever to invest in the market. Heck, you don't even need a broker anymore. You can hop online and start trading stocks or mutual funds completely on your own. As a result, costs to investors have fallen dramatically. Now, I don't want to say cost is everything. **Hedge funds** exist today that charge two-and-twenty (2 percent per year and 20 percent of annual profits) and still beat the returns in the most inexpensive of mutual funds. On the other hand, access to these types of funds are reserved for the ultra-wealthy, leaving the rest of us stuck with more traditional

> A HEDGE FUND IS BASICALLY A FANCY NAME FOR AN INVESTMENT PARTNERSHIP. IT'S THE MARRIAGE OF A PROFESSIONAL FUND MANAGER, WHO CAN OFTEN BE KNOWN AS THE GENERAL PARTNER, AND THE INVESTORS, SOMETIMES KNOWN AS THE LIMITED PARTNERS, WHO POOL THEIR MONEY TOGETHER INTO THE FUND.

market-based investments—typically with less annual returns, but also dramatically lower costs than ever before.

One area where the financial services industry finds the most fees? Mutual fund products of days past. The reality is that most investors don't know what they are actually paying in fees and expenses. In fact, a study conducted by TD Ameritrade of 1,000 investors found only 27 percent of Americans knew how much they were paying in 401(k) fees[23] as compared to the 95 percent of respondents who knew how much they were paying for streaming media services like Netflix and Hulu.[24] And the reality is, the fees in your mutual funds inside of your 401(k) are probably significantly more than the $5.99 or $7.99 a month you pay to these providers.

Not long ago, I had a retiree, Don, come to me for an independent scan of the annual fees and expenses he was paying his advisor. He worked with one of the most prestigious Registered Investment Advisory firms in the country at the time, where every dime he had was invested in mutual funds to the tune of $3,300,000. His investment advisory fees were 1 percent per year, in addition to the mutual fund expenses that averaged 1.36 percent per year (a bit lower than the average mutual fund fees we were seeing at the time). That brought his total costs to nearly $80,000 per year, though changes were rarely, if ever, made to the mutual fund holdings themselves. His portfolio contained some of the same mutual funds my 2-year-old son had in his **529 plan** at the time, with just a few thousand dollars. Why would someone with more than three million dollars invest the same way as a 2-year-old?

A 529 PLAN PROVIDES TAX ADVANTAGES WHEN SAVING AND PAYING FOR HIGHER EDUCATION. THERE ARE TWO MAJOR TYPES, PREPAID TUITION PLANS AND SAVINGS PLANS. PREPAID TUITION PLANS ALLOW THE PLAN HOLDER TO PAY FOR THE BENEFICIARY'S TUITION AND FEES AT DESIGNATED INSTITUTIONS IN ADVANCE. SAVINGS PLANS ARE TAX-ADVANTAGED INVESTMENT VEHICLES, SIMILAR TO IRAS.

The following chart illustrates the compounded effect of different fee levels, from a 1 percent fee to a 3 percent fee. The fees you pay matter and add up to potentially millions of dollars over time, much more than the few dollars you shell out for other expenses.

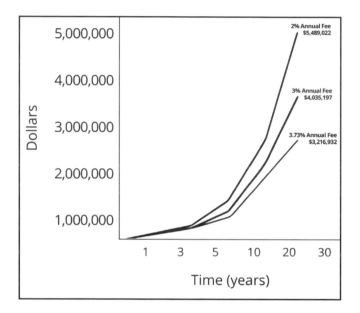

The reality is, someone with that kind of net worth certainly earned something better. There used to be a place for mutual funds and, in some cases, there still is. I would say those products are mostly for investors who are just getting started, though. For instance, my son only had around $5,000 in his 529 plan. To get diversification and professional money management, he had no choice but to use a mutual fund with limited transparency and higher fees.

There comes a time when you can transition to the institutionally managed world, the one that used to be reserved for the ultra-wealthy, much like the hedge-fund world. This is the way large institutions and trust funds manage their wealth. Do you think a multi-billion-dollar trust fund would invest in mutual funds? Of course not. Instead, they go to third-party money managers that assist them in managing their funds in accounts, holding securities specifically for their goals in mind. These investors place their money in stocks, bonds, index funds, and other individual holdings they will own themselves, rather than a pooled investment comprising hundreds or thousands of people across the country. This type demands complete transparency when it comes to not only their holdings, but their fees and expenses, as well.

Mutual Funds

One of the reasons brokers enjoy mutual funds is due to the lack of transparency regarding fees and expenses; it's much easier to keep clients invested when they don't see the annual fees and expenses coming directly out of their investment portfolio. Not only can you not see and feel the basic expenses (known as 12b 1 fees), but some expenses aren't even required to be disclosed, such as transaction costs. Every time there is something bought and sold in a mutual fund, it is passed through a brokerage and the fund pays a commission, which is not disclosed as part of the annual expenses of the fund. A study by Edelen, Evans and Kadlec found U.S. Stock Mutual Funds average 1.44 percent in transaction costs per year in addition to their average expense ratio of .90 percent, according to Morningstar.[25] With a third-party managed account, known as a Separately or Unified Managed Account, you have not only complete transparency in your exact holdings, but you can also see every fee and expense in your account as long as your money isn't pooled into investment vehicles, such as mutual funds. If you don't feel like your broker is performing well, you can at least see what the underperformance is costing you.

Another drag a mutual fund can place on your annual returns includes taxes. According to Morningstar, the average tax cost ratio for stock funds is 1 to 1.2 percent per year.[26] When purchasing a mutual fund, you are not purchasing the individual stocks inside of the fund. Instead, you are buying into the net asset value of the fund itself. This comes along with unrealized tax liabilities of the individual holdings inside of the fund, which, when realized, will be passed onto yourself. Many investors experienced the downside of this during the tech bubble of the 2000s.

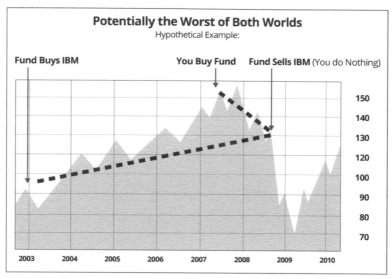

Source: Google Finance, circa 2014

If you were to purchase a mutual fund owning **IBM** stock after the major run-up in mutual funds leading up to the financial crisis, say in 2007, you would have experienced a loss in value of your original investment. However, since you purchased a fund with an unrealized gain, then that gain was passed onto you when it was sold, even though you didn't sell anything.

During this time, many funds were tech heavy and benefited from a dramatic rise in stock value through the '90s; the result— generating capital gains in many of the individual stock positions within the mutual funds themselves. If you were to buy into one of these funds toward the end of a bull run, such as the 1990s, and then go through a consequent downturn, panicked investors might liquidate their holdings, or the fund manager may decide to dump some of the holdings that had performed so well in days past. As a result, you would have to pay taxes on those gains, even though your investment in the mutual fund itself went down in value.

In contrast, if you invest in **Separate or Unified Managed Accounts**, you purchase the individual assets at whatever price they are at that time without undistributed tax liability—this results in much greater control over annual taxation and more money in your pocket over time.

Fees and Taxes

I don't want to understate the importance of fees and taxes when it comes to the growth side of your portfolio, but I also don't want to overstate them either—lest the tail wag the dog, so to speak. Sometimes, it might make sense to pay more for a sophisticated strategy with better potential or to take on additional taxable gains for an investment returning better after-tax returns than to pursue more tax-efficient investments.

A SEPARATED MANAGED ACCOUNT (SMA) IS A PORTFOLIO OF ASSETS MANAGED BY A PROFESSIONAL INVESTMENT FIRM. ONE OR MORE PORTFOLIO MANAGERS ARE RESPONSIBLE FOR DAY-TO-DAY INVESTMENT DECISIONS, SUPPORTED BY A TEAM OF ANALYSTS, OPERATIONS AND ADMINISTRATIVE STAFF.

A UNIFIED MANAGED ACCOUNT (UMA) IS A PROFESSIONALLY MANAGED PRIVATE INVESTMENT ACCOUNT THAT CAN INCLUDE MULTIPLE TYPES OF INVESTMENTS ALL IN A SINGLE ACCOUNT. INVESTMENTS MAY INCLUDE MUTUAL FUNDS, STOCKS, BONDS, AND EXCHANGE TRADED FUNDS. UNIFIED MANAGED ACCOUNTS ARE OFTEN REBALANCED ON A SPECIFIED SCHEDULE.

MEET TOM AND JANICE

Take, for instance, Tom and Janice. They were letting the tax tail wag the dog. They were 100 percent invested in municipal bonds to avoid taxes and fees. They could have received twice the rate of return on corporate bonds of similar quality and maturity. Although corporate bonds would have been taxable, their net return would be substantially higher than on tax-free municipal bonds—not to mention how shortsighted an investment strategy like that is when it comes to diversification. Again, while taxes are important, don't get blinded by the sales pitch—understand what the bottom line is for you personally before making any major financial decision. These are just other items to keep in the back of your mind while you are building the fiscal retirement home of your dreams!

Your Fiscal House

You can view The Purpose Based Retirement as a fiscal house, starting with the foundation. The foundation is the most important part of the house. In this case, it will consist of your emergency fund. Next, we have walls and the interior of the house representing your retirement income plan, which should be diverse. On the roof you will find your growth plan, where we begin to play defense against the eroding effects of inflation. Just as your roof will face some punishment from nature, so will your growth plan. Lastly, we put a fence around your assets, like you would around your home, to protect and ensure they pass on to those you love, as planned via a comprehensive estate plan.

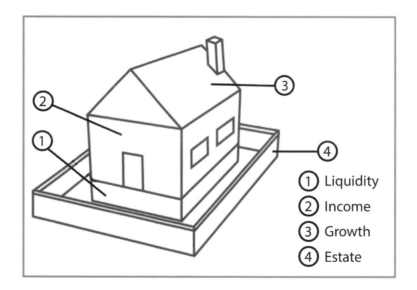

1. Liquidity
2. Income
3. Growth
4. Estate

CHAPTER 5: TAKEAWAYS, ACTIONS, AND NOTES

What are your biggest takeaways from this chapter?

_____

_____

_____

What are 3 action steps that you should work on now?

1. _____

2. _____

3. _____

What are 3 action steps for later?

1. _____

2. _____

3. _____

Notes:

_____

_____

_____

_____

_____

_____

CHAPTER SIX

ESTATE PLANNING

We may be ending your Purpose Based Asset Allocation with a discussion regarding estate planning, but this doesn't mean you should hold off on this planning until the very end! Quite the contrary; this is a key area of your overall financial plan—leaving it unaddressed has led to some of the greatest retirement disasters I have seen throughout my career. Consequences range from forcing retirees back to work, losing substantial portions of legacies to taxes, damaging family relationships, and even having whole estates default to unintended individuals.

Estate planning is the last piece of our Purpose Based Allocation, not because it lacks importance, but because we must prioritize as we structure our retirement strategy. Some may not have the assets necessary to cover all areas of planning and will choose to accept that risk (such as long-term health care), while others may choose to extend their working career to cover every major risk and wish.

Without an emergency fund, your retirement may be very short lived.

Without income, you don't have retirement.

Without inflation protection, you may not have the income you need later in life as the cost of living increases.

When it comes to estate planning, we are protecting assets as they pass on to our loved ones or protecting our estate from major health care expenses. Put another way, it comes down to disinheriting Uncle Sam and health care facilities to ensure there is something left for our beneficiaries in the end. This is a bigger priority for some than for others.

Many retirees put off thinking about the major health care risks they could face until it is too late. I see this most often with couples. It puts loved ones in a difficult situation at a very painful time in their lives.

MEET TOM AND MARGARET

There was once a widow, Margaret, who called our office in a panic following her first tax filing after the death of her husband the previous year. After more than 60 years of marriage, she had lost her husband, Tom, and was devastated. Not only was he the leader in their finances, but he also handled everything himself. There was limited communication between the couple regarding where their funds were, why they were there, and what to do in case something happened to him. He did a great job of investing over the years and held a large portion of their assets in non-qualified fixed annuities, due to his conservative nature. He owned these annuities for decades, benefitting from the tax deferral they offered—a feature I affectionately call "triple compounding," where the principal earns interest, the interest earns interest, and the taxes that would normally be paid annually also earn interest.

It worked great for Margaret and Tom, and by the time he died, the $500,000 they put in these fixed annuity contracts was worth over $1 million. When Tom passed away, Margaret went in to have a visit with their financial advisor, whom she had never met. At this point, Margaret was in her late 80s without a clue of what to do next. With Tom's passing, she was the sole owner of the annuities and she could move or withdraw funds. Her advisor recommended taking a full withdrawal of the contracts and instead invest in fee-based mutual funds, from which he would earn annual fees of 1.5

percent per year. By taking a lump sum distribution, all the gains in the annuities became taxable in a single year, costing her more than $150,000 in taxes on the annuity assets alone, not to mention taxes on Social Security and increases in Medicare premiums to boot.

If she hadn't taken a lump sum distribution, she could have withdrawn funds over time, distributing the taxable gains over an extended period.

Alternately, she could have annuitized the contracts, received payments over a certain period or even life and still cut her tax bill to a fraction of the amount.

This is just one example of a tax travesty that occurred primarily because there wasn't a proper estate plan in place to communicate Tom's wishes about their contracts. Even so, an estate plan can only go so far—open dialogue involving both spouses in the planning conversation can go miles further.

"...Ladies...your retirement could be 10, 15, 20 years longer than the man in your life. That is a huge, huge issue, so you've got to prepare for that. ...And here's what I would tell you, ladies, and I would say this to the husbands too, if you're married, imagine losing your spouse today and ask yourself what do you need to know about the money tomorrow? And the answer is everything."

~David Bach

This topic is incredibly important for women. Statistically speaking, women are more likely to be impacted by a lack of estate planning than men. The stories I share about legacy and estates often revolve around women because they are so often the ones left picking up the pieces. David Bach, author of *Smart Women Finish Rich*, explained at a conference I recently attended that most men will never know if the retirement plan they put in place ever works out, as their wives will most likely outlive them and find out on their own. I hope this helps illustrate how terribly important it is for both spouses to have a basic understanding of where things are and why. Sometimes, it's not as dramatic as it was for Margaret, but it can still be just as painful for the surviving spouse.

MEET BRENDA

Brenda came to visit us after the death of her husband, Michael. Prior to his death, she was told everything was set up and she would be fine. They had a couple hundred thousand dollars saved for retirement, along with a pension and Social Security income. They lived a happy and simple life. When Michael passed away, she lost the smaller of their two Social Security benefits—about a thousand dollars a month—and, unbeknownst to her, they had not selected survivors' benefits on her husband's pension. This meant $1,200 a month disappeared on top of her Social Security benefit. That left Brenda with just Michael's Social Security benefit (one thousand five hundred dollars per month) for a total monthly loss in income of almost 60 percent, or $2,200. Brenda's expenses were basically the same as before, but now she had about half as much income. She wanted to know how we could get her back to even. She would need to generate more than $25,000 a year from a $200,000 IRA and she was only 68 years old with great health. Realistically, Brenda would likely face a dramatic lifestyle change or risk running out of money.

MEET BARRY AND MARY ELLEN

In another example of estate planning blunders, our team implemented a retirement plan for a couple who decided to retire early—both in their early 60s. Barry and Mary Ellen wanted to take Social Security benefits and ride off into the sunset—or, pretty close. They wanted to move to the sunshine state of Florida. They were both avid golfers, cyclists and health food nuts. Seriously, they never even accepted a coffee when they came in for a visit with our team. Nothing but water! As we built out their Purpose Based Asset Allocation, they chose not to address long-term care risks, explaining they were both in excellent health and none of their family members had ever needed nursing home care in the past. Well, as the financial advisor's disclaimer reads, past performance is no guarantee of future results.

Shortly after retirement, Barry was teeing up on his favorite course in Florida when he had a sudden and unexpected stroke. He had no history of heart conditions, nor did anyone in his family. To say it was unexpected would be an understatement. He was rushed to the hospital, where his and his family's life would be forever changed.

Barry's doctors told him he was never going to leave a high-care medical facility again. His stroke had been severe; causing memory issues that inhibited his ability to care for himself, along with difficulty speaking. Other than his memory and speech issues, Barry was in relatively good health—probably due to all the regular physical activity he was involved in. The doctors said he could live for years, but he would not be able to take care of himself.

Mary Ellen tried to take care of him at home and did so successfully for a period of time, but the toll on her own health became too much. To this day, Barry still spends most of his time in an assisted living facility, for which Medicare offers no coverage. After the stroke, Barry and Mary Ellen's health care expenses quickly rose to more than $40,000 per year. Their emergency fund quickly depleted in the first few months of care, and their carefully crafted income strategy maxed out with additional income needs distributed from their long-term growth assets.

Mary Ellen called us almost immediately after the incident to ask what could be done. Unfortunately, it was too late; she would either be forced to dramatically reduce her monthly spending or risk running out of money before she was 75 years old.

It didn't have to be this way, though; prior to Barry's stroke, they had plenty of assets and discretionary income to structure a long-term care strategy that would have provided the benefits necessary to cover these expenses, but they chose to take the risk.

Regardless of your current health status or your family history, long-term health care needs can still cause financial devastation. For some families, their primary goal is to ensure they will never be a burden on their spouses or family members. For others, it is about preserving a legacy for the next generation or having the most choice regarding the quality of facility they end up utilizing. Regardless of the purpose, it is always a need that should be evaluated during the planning process and planned for if possible. Not all estate planning blunders result in financial loss. Sometimes, they drop mental hardships on the next generation.

MEET MY GRANDFATHER, HOWARD

My grandfather fell into this latter category. He never wanted to address what would happen upon his death; not even the most basic estate planning or pre-planning for his funeral. This may not seem like that big of a deal, but it burdened my grandmother and their two children with a great deal of unnecessary stress. Being forced to pick out the simplest of things, such as what my grandfather would wear and what type of casket to purchase, were just a couple extra things that had to be added to his loved ones' plates upon his death. It could have easily been avoided by not just pre-paying his funeral expenses, but pre-planning the funeral as well. It may not seem like much, but whatever can be done to lessen the burden and the number of decisions that need to be made upon death can make all the difference in the world.

MEET LISA

The lack of attention to simple beneficiary designations on policies and paperwork can have a huge impact on the children you leave behind as well. I once met with a woman named Lisa, who became the financial power of attorney for her father while he was still living. She opened investment accounts at a local bank to invest some of her father's cash when he reached his mid-90s. The not-so-good news: Lisa neglected to designate specified beneficiaries on this account prior to his death. On the other hand, her father already finalized a will designating her as the sole beneficiary of the estate. She was one of three siblings, but she assumed the responsibilities of caring for her dad in his old age, while her other two siblings remained estranged and had no relationship with their father. Upon the father's death, the will directed the courts to pass all assets on to his daughter, but her siblings contested the will. As a result, the assets did not get distributed for months due to litigation.

Ultimately, the courts fell back on the state "default" laws, distributing the account amongst all three children—against their father's wishes. Lisa told me that, while she didn't have a fantastic relationship with her siblings prior to their father's death, after his death they would most likely never speak again. The siblings felt she had coerced her father into making her the sole beneficiary of the estate. The drama could have been avoided with proper beneficiary designations.

The Importance Of Probate

Many families overlook the fact that your beneficiary designations will bypass **probate**, while your will is a probate document directing assets that are not designated by beneficiary. Essentially, your will is a letter to the judge, but can be contested upon death. Proper beneficiary designations may have salvaged whatever relationship she had with her siblings and at the very least kept these assets out of the court—saving thousands of dollars in attorney fees along the way.

PROBATE IS A LEGAL PROCESS IN WHICH A WILL IS REVIEWED TO DETERMINE WHETHER IT IS VALID AND AUTHENTIC. PROBATE ALSO REFERS TO THE GENERAL ADMINISTERING OF A DECEASED PERSON'S WILL OR THE ESTATE OF A DECEASED PERSON WITHOUT A WILL.

It's important to plan for what you want to happen to your assets after you're gone. One component of this includes the need to be able to have discussions with your loved ones about your wishes while you still can. For some families, this is an easy, open and ongoing discussion. For others, it may be best to schedule a formal occasion in which to discuss planning. In my observation, though, the families who are kept most up-to-date and in the loop about estate planning are the ones who make it through the passing of the older generation most intact. Part of this is because shedding light on factors such as who will execute the will or who inherits the house from a parent face-to-face is often easier for siblings than to find out that so-and-so will be handling the estate transfer after the fact. Truly, planning early and being open about it can preserve much more than just a monetary legacy.

Basic Documents

As you can see, estate planning isn't all about working with a qualified estate planning attorney to structure appropriate documentation. It's about much more than just having the right paperwork in place. This is not to say these important documents should be overlooked in any way—quite the contrary. Your basic estate planning documents will be the foundation of your overall estate planning strategy. Yet, the degree of an estate's complexity can vary greatly from one family to the next, depending on their wishes, family structure and the size of the estate itself. Most families are able to get their needs covered through minor legal fees and, in many cases, these documents can be completed inexpensively online rather than with a local estate planning attorney. When my wife and I had our first child, we didn't have substantial savings or business entities. Consequently, we just needed some basic estate planning. I hopped online and knocked out the most vital documents at minimal cost. As our business grew along with our savings, things became more complicated and we needed to hire an estate planning attorney. However simple or complex your situation, you will need the basics at a minimum. The basics that should cover most every family include a last will and testament, powers of attorney, and a living will.

Last Will and Testament

Your last will and testament are essentially a catch-all document designating how you would like your property and assets distributed upon your death. Essentially, this is a letter to the probate judge. It will assist in directing assets without beneficiary designations attached to them pass to those you wish them to, as well as designating an executor to ensure what you have specified will be carried out, in addition to naming guardians for any minor children you may have.

Powers Of Attorney

Powers of attorney can be divided into two basic categories: health care and financial power of attorney. It is a good idea to split these powers between individuals to avoid any potential conflicts of interest. A financial power of attorney allows you to designate someone to manage the financial decisions of your estate if you are unable to do so yourself. A health care power of attorney allows you to designate someone to make medical decisions on your behalf if you can't make them for yourself. Personally, I designated my father as my health care power of attorney and wife as my financial power of attorney. I didn't want my wife to have to make difficult medical decisions that are in our family's best financial and psychological interest, but I knew my father could make these difficult decisions if he had to.

Living Will

A living will, also sometimes referred to as a health care proxy, ensures your wishes regarding medical care are followed in the event you become terminally ill and need to be on a life support system. A living will is only applicable if you are terminally ill or permanently unconscious. For this reason, it is wise to have both a living will and a designated health care power of attorney. A health care power of attorney will be responsible for managing health care decisions that may result from a temporary state of unconsciousness or inability to communicate, but not necessarily direct major decisions if you are terminally ill, in a permanently vegetative state or another end-stage condition. In some states, the living will and health care powers of attorney are combined into a single document that may also cover other various matters, such as designation of a primary physician, desires regarding the donation of body organs and whom you would like appointed as your legal guardian if the need arises.

Trust

The preceding documents took care of my family's needs until the size of our estate grew to a point that I had greater concerns regarding the control of assets beyond the grave. Not only do I have to plan for my personal estate, but my wife and I must tie up the details pertaining to the various business entities we own and operate. As a result, we structured a revocable living trust.

While most individuals can simply use proper beneficiary designation in place of a trust to ensure assets avoid probate, families often use trusts to avoid probate. For our family, we had greater concerns regarding control over substantial financial and business assets passing to our children at a young age. The trust allowed us to establish goals and incentives for our children to gain control over the assets they would be left with in the case of our death—including educational, income, and age earmarks for distribution. Sometimes this is referred to as a goal-based trust.

The most common error with a revocable trust is keeping it funded in the first place. All assets that are intended to become part of the trust upon death should be owned by the trust prior to death, if possible. Otherwise, they will still become probate-able upon death. While it is not necessary to have a lawyer involved to establish a trust, this document is typically only a requirement for more complex estate planning situations, which may be best handled via legal counsel.

A trust is a legal framework that allows an entity, such as a person or bank, to hold assets and transfer them from a trustor or grantor to the trustee. In our legal system, these can be revocable; meaning the trustor retains control over the assets during their lifetime, or irrevocable; once the trustor puts assets in, they can't get them out. Trusts can be used to pass on money to minors, holding the assets until the child comes of age, or they can even be used to put other stipulations on the beneficiaries. Trusts can come in particularly handy for blended families, families with special needs children who will need care, or families with specific charitable goals.

MEET ROBERT AND HELEN

An example of someone who greatly benefited from a trust structure was a couple who had nearly $2 million in a single bank stock. Robert and Helen had a total net worth of just under $3 million. They relied on the dividend income from that stock to pay their bills in retirement, but recognized they were taking a great deal of risk due to this highly concentrated holding. They didn't know what else to do. They inherited the bank stock decades prior and it had appreciated greatly over time, with unrealized gains of over $1 million. If they were to sell the stock and diversify, the tax hit would cost them so much of their net worth, they would no longer be able to generate dividends at the same level moving forward to cover their expenses. They had no children and planned to pass all their assets to various charities. We worked with an attorney to establish a charitable trust, allowing them to contribute the stock to the trust.

Once inside the trust, Robert and Helen could liquidate and diversify the concentrated stock position without tax consequences. In addition, due to the nature of their trust with their favorite charities as trustees, they would receive a charitable deduction they could use against their taxable income into the future. This allowed them to gain much greater peace of mind. By pursuing the diversification and structure of a REAL income strategy, they could pick up tax deductions while still living, as opposed to tax benefits that would only benefit their estate after death.

MEET DAN AND JOANNA

In another instance, we worked with a couple who had a special needs daughter. She was their only daughter and was in her 30s at the time. While the couple wanted to leave her all their assets after death, they were afraid she would lose her government-provided benefits if those assets ended up in her name. They weren't rich—they only had a couple hundred thousand dollars to leave behind. But they knew if their daughter lost government assistance, she would be penniless in a short period of time due to her medical expenses and inability to provide for herself. A special needs trust would allow them to leave assets behind that could be doled out over time, allowing her to receive some financial benefit and still maintain her government assistance. In addition, it could minimize her access to the funds, allaying their concerns about her possibly spending the inheritance irresponsibly, commonly known as spendthrift provisions. This trust gave the couple the peace of mind to know their daughter, who had depended on them her entire life, would still be taken care of after they were gone.

MEET JOE

Sometimes, the reason for more advanced estate planning is to maximize the legacy of abnormally large estates and avoid unnecessary taxation. I remember Joe, who was single but had a girlfriend he had been with for decades. Joe had more money than he could ever spend, with nearly $10 million in various types of investments. He accumulated so much in part because he was incredibly frugal—he proudly drove the same Chevy Impala to our office for years, saying he had more than 200,000 miles on it. Knowing he wasn't going to be able to spend all his life savings, he recognized a well-defined purpose for most of these funds: maximize their after-tax return for his girlfriend and siblings. With an estate of that size, and being a single individual, his estate was staring at a very significant tax upon his passing. Over time, we moved funds into an irrevocable trust that would fund a life insurance policy offering a guaranteed tax-free return on his deposits. On death, his current estate would double in size. The trust allowed us to minimize Joe's estate and income taxes while leveraging his insurability. He said it was a great weight lifted off his shoulders—knowing exactly what he was going to leave behind and that it couldn't be squandered due to trust provisions. It would go to exactly who he wanted it to and, ultimately, he would have an impact or legacy. He always said he wanted to be a good steward of his life savings and putting in place a Purpose Based Retirement Plan did just that.

If you fall into one of these more complex categories, you will undoubtedly need to meet with an estate planning attorney to discuss your estate planning strategy.

Long-Term Health Care Risks

While most want to avoid any discussion regarding death, even fewer want to address the potential risk of winding up with a long-term health care need during retirement. When most of us think of long-term health care expenses, we often think of gloomy nursing homes with poor staff and unhappy patients.

MEET MY GRANDMOTHER, CHRISTINE

I know this experience well. My grandmother, Christine Weade, required skilled nursing care. Toward the end of her life, she suffered from congestive heart failure and dementia. I was very close to my grandmother growing up, so it was very difficult to see her in this condition. Initially, a stroke landed her in the local hospital. I went to visit her as soon as I could, which wasn't easy in the middle of a blizzard. I walked into her room, hopped into her hospital bed, threw my arm around her and held her close. I was later reprimanded by the nurse for this, and hers weren't the only feathers ruffled by my gesture of familiarity.

My grandfather passed a few years prior, and my grandmother decided to start dating again. As I lay in the hospital bed with my grandmother, her boyfriend walked in. I will never forget the look on his face when he saw me there. We hadn't met before, and this old gentleman quickly turned away and left the room upon seeing a strapping young guy in bed with his lady—a look of disgust on his face. He later confronted my grandmother, wanting to know who that guy was in bed with her. My grandmother was a pretty lively old lady and gave him heck for even questioning her.

My grandmother seemed to have trouble remembering who visited her early in the day, so I asked the nurse if she felt it was a sign of Alzheimer's. The nurse told me it was difficult to say at this point, but as time went on, it became clear that she was suffering continual difficulty with her memory. Eventually, after further heart trouble and ongoing memory issues (including not being able to remember to take her medication), she ended up in a skilled nursing care facility.

One day, I remember visiting her with my wife, Chelsie. When we came to visit, it said "Welcome, Christine" on her whiteboard in the room. My wife remarked, "That's really sweet of them to welcome you, they must be really nice here." Grandma replied to ask if we could instead cross it out to say, "Goodbye, Christine." She hated it in that nursing home, and I couldn't blame her. It was a sad place to live, and I desperately wanted to get her out. That day, my father called to ask if I was going to visit Grandma sometime soon. I told him we spent a few hours there earlier, but my father had just spoken with her on the phone, and she told him she hadn't seen me in weeks.

A few days later, she enlisted her boyfriend to break her out of the nursing home. He put her in a wheelchair and tried to load her up in his truck for takeoff. It was quite a fiasco, but it gives one the idea of how much she hated it there. Fortunately, she didn't have to be there for long; my spunky grandmother passed away a few weeks after her failed break-out attempt. Given my own grandmother's experience, I understand why people are so reluctant to address the subject of long-term care, but it's important to understand that not all long-term care experiences are negative.

MEET BRIAN AND SHEILA

I once worked with one of the most adorable couples I have ever come across. Sheila was always right by Brian's side, holding his arm or walking hand in hand as they entered the office. You could tell how much they adored one another. She was interested in cars and loved her '69 Camaro—it was always a topic of conversation when we were together. She almost loved it as much as the jewelry her husband gifted to her just to see her smile. They retired a year before we first met and implemented their Purpose Based Retirement. Five years later, she began to forget things. At first, it was the simplest things; where she put the keys or how long she left the lasagna in the oven. The casual observer wouldn't have known it—she seemed as sharp as ever whenever we got together to review their plan.

That soon changed, though. One day, she didn't join us for our review. I immediately asked about it. Sheila never missed an opportunity to spread her hugs and kisses around our office. Brian shared that her condition was getting worse and the doctors diagnosed her with early onset Alzheimer's. I couldn't believe it; she was always the sharpest of the two, but now she could no longer remember who I was or where she was. The doctors told Brian she needed to be under 24-hour care; she couldn't be left alone. At one point, he would take Sheila to adult day care a few times a week, which she thought was great. It was the happiest time of her day, as she assumed she was back in school again. As time went on, Brian's health and ability to care for her waned. He could no longer provide the level of care she needed. It broke his heart, but Sheila had to move to an assisted living facility.

I was so sad for him at first, but the day after he moved her in, he had a smile on his face. He said, "She's happier than I've seen her in months, she's surrounded by friends and even people she knows. There's always something to do and I just couldn't provide her with that." Sheila loved to dance and socialize, and there was always something going on. Her favorite thing was that the facility gave residents the opportunity to take dance lessons—one of her favorite things to do with Brian.

This allowed Brian to get some of his own life back, as well. He hadn't been able to visit their children and grandchildren for years since Sheila could not travel. Now, he planned trips to go see them on a regular basis. He was even able to restore his golf game a bit and go on the occasional fishing trip. Of course, Brian never left Sheila for long. If he wasn't traveling, he was by her side just trying to make her smile. All of this wouldn't have been possible without the long-term care strategies we put in place as they stepped into retirement. Thankfully, they are both happy and able to continue enjoying the time they have left together years into the future.

The odds of needing long-term health care at some point during retirement for those over the age of 65 is around 70 percent. Those odds sound high because they are. If it's hard to believe, maybe it's important for us to define just exactly what long-term health care really is. Long-term health care isn't just nursing home care. It includes a continuum of medical and social services designed to support the needs of people living with chronic health problems, which affect their ability to perform everyday activities. These services include three levels of care: in-home, assisted and skilled nursing health care needs. There are different odds of needing each level of care, as well. While the odds of requiring some form of long-term health care are around 70 percent, the odds of needing skilled nursing home care are around 40 percent for those aged 65.[27] Still, skilled nursing home care is the most likely insurance claim you will probably face during retirement. The length of the average stay in a skilled nursing care facility is around two-and-a-half years, with an average cost of around $90,000 per year nationally in 2018, according to Genworth. That's around $225,000 for the average stay with about a 50-50 shot of occurrence.[28]

I think it's safe to say we should be having a discussion regarding needs and options at the onset of any truly comprehensive retirement plan—especially if you might face a risk that's just as likely as a financial emergency, market crash or inflation during your retirement.

Once we face reality, we must ask, what are our options for payment? While Medicare may cover your expenses for a short period of time, up to one hundred days of care in some instances, beyond that you are on your own. That means any payments come directly out of your pocket until you qualify for Medicaid. Qualification for Medicaid varies state by state but, regardless, to qualify you must spend your own assets first. Medicaid is for those who are financially impoverished, and, qualifying for it takes many decisions out of your hands when it comes to the facility and level of care you receive. For instance, home health care, which most families would prefer, is typically out of the question.

Outside of those options, which don't sound all that appealing, we must evaluate some form of long-term care insurance. Despite what you may think, there are many different ways to get long-term care coverage. Some policies come with a traditional insurance premium, while others are asset-based in nature, and may or may not require medical qualification. Let's cover some of these major forms of coverage and their pros and cons next.

Traditional Long-Term Care Insurance

Traditional long-term care insurance is like most other insurance coverages that you are used to paying, such as your health, property and casualty insurance. You will pay an annual premium for a specified level of benefits, and it's typically use it or lose it. Insurance companies greatly underestimated the demand that would be placed upon their reserves when these products initially launched. As a result, premiums increased dramatically on these insureds and many insurance companies either exited the long-term care insurance business or were put out of business altogether.

This understandably created a tremendous amount of negative news coverage. Premiums have reached unaffordable levels for most consumers and, as such, traditional long-term care insurance policies are rarely used to fund long-term care needs in comparison to its heyday. Rates and benefits are always evolving, so this should still be evaluated as a potential long-term care solution. It's important to not dismiss any option out of hand without kicking the tires first, so to speak. In addition, some employers may offer discounted long-term care solutions at a much more affordable price. For instance, I had a client who was evaluating long-term care insurance policies and I recommended we first check with his human resources department to see if his employer offered a viable solution. Luckily, he had access to a policy that would only cost $600 per year for $250,000 dollars in benefits — adjusted annually for inflation. A similar product with a private insurer could cost thousands of dollars per year for equivalent benefits.

Asset-Based Life Insurance Solutions

The gentleman in the preceding example was married, and his wife unfortunately didn't have the same kind of employer-subsidized policy available. For her, we decided to explore an asset-based solution. They had an overflow emergency fund of $100,000 sitting at the bank. From that, they moved $75,000 to a product that would earn minimal interest, slightly better than the bank. They could get their money back at any time, and if they had a long-term care need, this product would provide similar benefits to the husband's employer-based plan. This would not require any on-going premiums, but instead just a re-arranging of assets. They never planned on using that emergency fund, but it was there if they needed it. One of the ironic things is that the circumstance for which they would most likely have used their emergency fund was a long-term health care event. Now, it was still available for any number of reasons, but they had extra benefits for long-term care needs. Additionally, if they never used the money, the long-term care benefits would pass on as a tax-free death benefit to their heirs.

As I mentioned before, it's about finding the closest distance between two points; a straight line, to maximize the efficiency of the dollars you have saved for retirement. This couple's emergency money was arranged most efficiently for their purpose—adding value without adding cost. On the other hand, if they were willing to give up control of the funds entirely, we could have provided even greater benefits. In this instance, however, they would have lost their overflow emergency fund due to penalties and/or costs that could eat into the cash deposit.

MEET MICHAEL AND SUSAN

In some instances, riders can be attached to these asset-based plans, providing extended benefits for a minimal annual premium. For example, Michael and Susan had an IRA they did not need for retirement income. We already satisfied the first three areas of their Purpose Based Retirement Allocation and were left with additional IRA funds, which they knew they would be forced to take RMDs from—RMDs they did not need. These additional required distributions would cause frustrating taxation. Still, that could all be smoothed out if they began taking distributions now rather than later when the account was larger (a larger balance would require larger taxable distributions).

Michael and Susan decided to take small annual distributions from the account over a period of ten years and move the funds into an asset-based, long-term care policy, satisfying both of their long-term care needs. In addition, we attached a rider that they would need to pay for separately out of their monthly cash flow but allow for benefits to continue as long as they needed long-term care—even after the benefit pool was used up. This not only filled their most likely needs but provided additional reassurance. Regardless of how long they needed the care they would have coverage. It also allowed for a tax-free death benefit to pass onto the heirs should they be lucky enough not to need long-term care.

Traditional Life Insurance Policies With Accelerated Death Benefit Provisions

Life insurance solutions have evolved tremendously over the years, providing more benefits at a lower and more predictable cost than in years past. Many permanent policies also include provisions that allow you to have "living benefits." These provide you with the ability to spend down your death benefit even while you are alive for qualifying events, such as long-term care or disability needs. This is the solution I have chosen for myself and my father's long-term care solutions.

For myself, I needed to have traditional life insurance to protect my family's financial well-being in case of my death. When I purchased my life insurance policies, I used policies that have provisions to accelerate paying out a death benefit while I'm living in case of critical, chronic and/or terminal illness. These policies also doubled as a disability benefit solution in case I become disabled. When I evaluated traditional long-term disability insurance, it seemed extremely expensive. In addition, I knew I could potentially be throwing thousands of dollars down the drain should I never use the policy benefits, which is how most retirees feel about traditional long-term care insurance. As such, I could pay for term insurance to cover temporary needs, including debt and expenses at a younger age. At the same time, I could use cash-value based life insurance policies as a source of tax-free retirement income if I didn't need to use the death benefit prior for disability and/or health care expenses.

In the case of my father, he was divorced when we picked out coverage. That was important, because we want to identify the reason for the coverage in the first place. In many cases, long-term care coverage is picked up not to just protect the estate, but to ensure the healthy spouse is not left destitute with major long-term health care expenses for the spouse who needs care. In my dad's case, he had plenty of assets to self-insure and pay for those expenses out of pocket; I was the one who would be left essentially footing the bill with my inheritance.

My father built a beautiful home in Asheville, North Carolina that he absolutely loved. One day, I remember him sending me pictures of the sun rising over the mountains followed up by a phone call in which he said, "Someday, son, this will be yours." I said, "You're right, as long as we don't have to sell it to pay for the nursing home," laughing, of course. He offered a flippant response, saying the only way that would ever happen is if he couldn't find the gun. Of course, he recognized if he needed nursing home care, he probably wouldn't be able to find the gun in the first place. I decided to purchase a $500,000 life insurance policy on him. There was no reason for him to purchase the policy himself, since he had assets he could use to pay for potential care. I purchased it as an investment in my inheritance and as a guaranteed tax-free return for my annual savings. It would accelerate the death benefit in case he needed long-term care coverage and would ultimately pay out a tax-free death benefit on his passing regardless of his long-term care need.

In many instances, I run into clients who have old, active life insurance policies they plan to pass to their children someday; many with substantial cash values they don't need for retirement. These cash values will be left to the insurance company, ultimately with the life insurance company itself only needing to pay out the difference between the cash value in the policy and the death benefit. Let me map this out. I met with a couple whose life insurance policy contained cash value that would allow for the death benefit to stay in-force for the rest of their lives, and without any further premiums. We exchanged the old policy for a new one while maintaining the same cash values and death benefit. Now, though, the new policy would also allow them to utilize the death benefit in case of a long-term care need. It didn't cost them anything to make the exchange, but they picked up benefits they would not have had otherwise.

After stress-testing their overall plan following this simple move, we found a small gap of long-term care needs that could be filled with a low-cost, low-benefit traditional long-term care insurance policy. In other instances, we may choose to give up the cash value in the policy for a bigger death and long-term care benefit. This is because you may never plan to use the cash value for your own purposes, anyway. If you let the cash value ride idle without utilizing it to purchase a bigger death benefit, then the insurance carrier only must pay out the difference between the cash value and the specified death benefit. That means you foot the bill for the rest. Get that cash value to work and don't let them just slide it in their pocket when you've left this mortal plane.

Asset-Based Annuities With Long-Term Care Riders

One of the biggest downsides to traditional long-term care insurance or even life insurance with accelerated death benefit provisions is the requirement that the insured pass a health exam. Many people seeking long-term care coverage of some kind may be of an age or health history that makes this insurance unlikely or unaffordable. In this case, you may want to evaluate annuities with long-term care riders that do not require you to pass a medical exam and are not necessarily age dependent.

MEET RICHARD AND LUCY

Richard and Lucy were very serious about long-term care concerns. They watched Lucy's mother deplete all her retirement assets to pay for nursing home care. Sadly, Richard's multiple bouts with cancer made him nearly uninsurable via long-term care insurance or traditional life insurance policies. The few policies they qualified for were prohibitively expensive due to their age. Instead, they turned to annuities that had guaranteed lifetime withdrawal benefit (GLWB) riders with long-term care provisions. The guaranteed income benefits would satisfy Richard and Lucy's retirement income needs for the rest of their lives. If either of them needed long-term health care, the guaranteed income benefits they were using to meet their monthly spending needs would double for a period of five years. After that, the income would drop back to their original guaranteed income benefit for the remainder of their lives. This satisfied the most likely level of care they would encounter should they need it. The annuity Richard and Lucy purchased would pay out following a long-term care need that persisted beyond 90 days if a physician verified they could not perform two out of six activities of daily living (ADLs). It would also cover all three levels of care: home health care, assisted living and skilled nursing care. The benefits of these contracts will vary, so be sure you pay attention to elimination periods and the type of coverage that will qualify for benefit payout.

For more information on how to account for long-term care, check out the Educational Videos section of the Howard Bailey website; particularly the "Understanding Long Term Care Options" video: https://howardbailey.com/educational-videos/long-term-care-options/

Legacy Maximization

So far, we have discussed how you can implement a basic estate plan, ensure your assets will pass to your loved ones as efficiently as possible, and preserve those assets from major long-term care expenses. Now, we must turn our attention to ensuring Uncle Sam is cut out of the picture. The last thing you need is to make Uncle Sam the biggest beneficiary of your life savings. He may need the financial assistance, but you should never leave too much to someone who's that fiscally irresponsible.

Basic Ira Strategies

One of the biggest liabilities most retirees will face is the tax-deferred benefit accounts they have accrued over their lifetimes. This mainly consists of individual retirement accounts (IRAs) and 401(k)s, in addition to other employer-sponsored retirement plans. These assets are not only taxable upon distribution to yourself, but also to your heirs upon death. Some of the most basic planning starts with determining how to best distribute these tax-deferred accounts upon your death.

Stretch IRA

IRAs, often retirees' largest assets, can be troublesome for survivors because of their precarious tax situation. As deferred assets, IRAs have never been taxed, and Uncle Sam is determined to get his portion. For a surviving spouse, inheriting an IRA is as easy as replacing the original owner's name with your own or even rolling those assets into your existing IRA.

Regardless of to whom or how an IRA is passed on, the recipient will pay required minimum distributions and their accompanying income taxes at whatever the beneficiary's highest marginal tax rate is. This is where a technique called a "stretch" comes into play. Since RMDs are based on life expectancy, the younger a beneficiary, the lower the RMD. To help make these assets multi-generational, some families will even skip a generation to name a grandchild as the beneficiary and avoid the higher required minimum distributions that would be due on their immediate children due to a shorter life expectancy.

Let's see how this might work. Say Jacob and Eunice have several healthy retirement assets, including an IRA with a lot of untaxed assets built up. Their son, David, is in his late 40s and making the most money he's ever made in his life. David and his wife are probably in the highest tax bracket they will ever be in—not an ideal time to have to start taking RMDs and paying the associated taxes. David has no need for the IRA funds because in addition to his own assets, he stands to inherit the bulk of his parents' estate when they pass on. But David's daughter, Gloria, is just getting out of college. If Jacob and Eunice were to name Gloria as the beneficiary of their IRA, the RMDs would be much smaller since they would be based on Gloria's lifespan, and Gloria's taxable income is much lower to boot.

In this way, a family can allow more money to stay in the account and grow. A strategy like this could stretch a sizeable asset across multiple generations, all without incurring a hefty tax bill.

Roth Conversion

You may be saying, "Wait a minute, Casey, I thought Roth IRAs didn't have RMDs." You're right. During the lifetime of the owner, Roth IRAs don't have RMDs. Yet, after the original account owner has passed, the beneficiaries must withdraw RMDs calculated on their own life expectancy. Unlike traditional IRA RMDs, though, Roth IRA RMDs are still income-tax-free. If you recall in a previous chapter, we discussed converting as much of your traditional IRA into a Roth IRA as possible before RMDs kick in. When it comes to legacy planning, another question to ask is: even after you are 70 ½ and have begun taking RMDs, are you still in a lower income tax bracket than your likely heirs? If so, it might still be worth converting your traditional IRA—even at a higher tax bracket for you—into a Roth account, saving taxes for your beneficiaries down the road.

Another consideration is, just like with traditional IRAs, since Roth account RMDs are based on the lifespan of the inheriting owner, you may consider stretching a Roth over multiple generations by making a younger generation the beneficiary. This permits the assets inside to continue compounding their growth tax-free for an extended period of time due to smaller required distributions that would be required of an older generational beneficiary.

Distribution Strategies

In addition to stretching your IRAs upon death and converting them to Roth IRAs, you may want to consider ways of creating a more substantial tax-free death benefit for your heirs through the use of a life insurance strategy.

My dad is currently doing this with his nonqualified tax-deferred annuities, but the strategy can also apply to systematic distributions for tax-deferred retirement plans. In my family, legacy has been very important, starting with my grandfather leaving my father a modest sum of money. My dad has the goal of passing this inheritance down and adding to it for the next generation. I also have the same goal. He knows that during retirement he will likely be in a lower tax bracket than I will be when I ultimately inherit those tax-deferred assets. So, as he distributes those tax-deferred assets over time, he is re-depositing them into tax-free life insurance policies that will offer a guaranteed, tax-free rate of return. They will also immediately offer substantially more benefits than would ever be seen from the tax-deferred annuities he is using to pay for the policies. In his case, he is only insuring himself, but in other cases we are working with couples that want to maximize their legacy for their next generation together.

Leveraging the lives of two individuals allows us substantially more in benefits than just one individual through survivorship (a.k.a. second-to-die) life insurance strategies. These types of policies will not pay out until the death of both individuals. As such, the insurance company can get more predictability regarding life expectancy, offering more leverage for larger death benefits. One couple I worked with had goals of maximizing the legacy they would leave behind, as we more than satisfied their other needs in the first three areas of their Purpose Based Asset Allocation.

We used portions of their RMDs to purchase traditional life insurance with accelerated death benefit provisions as their long-term care solution. We also used excess assets to fund a survivorship life insurance policy offering four times the death benefits that could be achieved when insuring only a single life. The neat thing about their survivorship policy is that it also came with an accelerated death benefit provision for long-term health care needs. The accelerated benefits could only be paid out after the death of the first insured, which was in line with their wishes. They expect the first person to need long-term care will have substantial assistance from their spouse. After one spouse dies, the remaining person may be at higher risk of needing institutional care because they will not have a spouse to rely on. The most liberating part of this strategy was they recreated the entire current size of their estate with the survivorship life insurance policy. They knew that if they spent all their other assets, they would still leave behind the same amount of assets they had on day one of the plan through the survivorship policy death benefit.

This couple previously felt apprehensive about spending their money. They wanted to ensure they did not spend the principal they hoped to leave to their heirs. Now, they could spend with the confidence of knowing if they spent everything else, which would still be unlikely, they would preserve the current assets they had at the onset of the strategy. This strategy can be very advantageous to couples at odds over what they want to leave behind for the next generation. Many times, couples have different ideas of what the purpose of their life savings really is. While one may feel no responsibility to leave behind a legacy for the next generation, the other may feel very strongly about financially benefiting those they leave behind. I will often sit with couples in our first strategy visits and hear them discover just how different their goals are.

MEET DON AND LORI

Once, I worked with a lovely couple, Don and Lori, on their Purpose Based Retirement strategy. They did a great job of saving for retirement. They weren't big earners, but they were tremendous savers. We filled each of their required Purpose Based Allocations and still had funds left over to put toward a substantial legacy. I sensed some angst coming from Lori's side of the table and asked how she felt about our direction. She said she didn't understand why they worked their whole lives, pinched their pennies and sacrificed just so they could leave it all behind—and then some to their children. Lori felt that they had done enough already, since she and Don had raised their kids, put them through school and helped them buy their first home. Don, though, felt it was an obligation they owed to the next generation.

As we dug deeper, it became apparent that Don harbored some resentments from his own experiences. You see, his parents spent their life savings and, later in life, not only did they have nothing monetarily to leave behind, but their circumstances forced their children—including Don—to shoulder many of their financial burdens. In a certain sense, Don wanted to make up for his parents' shortcomings—something Lori hadn't realized was still burdening him. Using a Purpose Based Retirement, though, Don and Lori found a compromise that allowed them to have their cake and eat it, too.

Inheritances: IRA and 401(k)

A final word on IRA and 401(k) inheritances: if you have RMDs you don't need, in addition to triggering taxes on Social Security and increasing your Medicare premiums, you may also consider the ongoing tax implications of where you put those dollars once they come out of your IRA. If you have no need for the dollars and ultimately expect to pass them onto your heirs, it might make more sense to reallocate them to life insurance policies on which *you* and your heirs will not be taxed.

For more on this topic, check out the Educational Videos
section of the Howard Bailey website and watch our video,
"Using Tax Buckets in a Retirement Strategy,"

https://howardbailey.com/educational-videos/tax-buckets/

Annuity Legacy Strategies

If you still aspire to maximize the guaranteed legacy for your
heirs, but don't qualify for some of the previously discussed life
insurance strategies due to age or health, it may behoove you to
evaluate annuity death benefit strategies that don't require health
exams or ongoing premiums.

Along these lines, I once had a retiree who had no goals of
spending down her IRA and had no need for the annual RMDs. In
addition, she was in her early seventies and had a heart condition
that made her unlikely to qualify for life insurance. Instead, we used
an annuity contract that guaranteed her account would continue to
grow in terms of death benefits, even as she satisfied the minimum

distribution requirements. She had peace of mind that her RMDs would never eat into her principal.

In another case, we met with a gentleman in his late seventies who was not in the best of health. As a result, we were able to allocate his funds to an account with a substantial upfront bonus. He passed away two years later, but the principal and bonus enabled additional dollars to pass to the next generation—more so than going the route of taking on substantial market risk over the same period.

Annuity death benefits come in many forms; sometimes as upfront bonuses, guaranteed growth rates, daily step-ups in value due to market returns and even multiples of market returns. The downside is that annuities do not pass tax-free to your heirs unless they are held inside a Roth IRA. As such, life insurance is the more attractive option, if available. The correct option for you and your family will be dependent on factors that include your age, tax qualification of the account, your health, risk tolerance and general financial situation.

The downside of annuity death benefits is the tax-deferred nature of these accounts—where gains will be taxable upon death. Fortunately, most annuities provide the ability (or, sometimes, it's a requirement) to distribute funds over a period of time. This stretches out the taxation of these assets and minimizes the overall tax impact. In some instances, I found that retirees with spendthrift children appreciate the additional incentive for responsible spending offered by the stretching of these funds over a period of time. For those without tolerance or time for market volatility to run its course, an annuity with a death benefit rider can be a valid solution.

CHAPTER 6: TAKEAWAYS, ACTIONS, AND NOTES

What are your biggest takeaways from this chapter?

_____

_____

_____

What are 3 action steps that you should work on now?

1. _____

2. _____

3. _____

What are 3 action steps for later?

1. _____

2. _____

3. _____

Notes:

_____

_____

_____

_____

_____

_____

CLOSING

When to start: Ahh—the age-old question of when to begin planning for retirement. It bewilders me that this is even a question. When should you begin saving, or paying off your debt or setting yourself up for a career, for that matter? We're talking about your future here. We should be planning for this in some form or another from the moment we are conscious that it is a need. Why wait for something that is inevitably going to come if we live long enough, which we all hope to, in the first place? We must always be planning with a purpose.

Money without a purpose is just a dollar sign, and accumulating wealth should always have a more powerful purpose behind it or you will be left unfulfilled.

Of course, there are different things to focus on at different stages of your financial life, but all should have the goal of creating financial security, and not just for the short-term.

Let's start by looking at each stage, what your focus should be and what type of financial professional you should be working with, if any. I've seen some financial life cycle breakdowns that involved as many as ten or more phases of financial life. However, there are really two areas of focus for most financial professionals: the accumulation phase and the spend-down phase of retirement.

COMPETING PRIORITIES

	Accumulation Advisor	Retirement Advisor
First Priority	Growth	Income
Second Priority	Safety	Safety
Third Priority	Income	Growth

While most financial professionals have the same priorities, the order of those priorities differs based on what kind of advisor they are.

Accumulation

In the accumulation stage, you may be just starting out, or perhaps you are well into your career. The good thing is you have time on your side before you need the funds you are saving. Your focus will most likely begin with paying down debt and transitioning into saving as much as possible out of every paycheck while still living comfortably. This is the stage at which very few individuals really need a financial advisor in the first place. Your goal is to accumulate as much as possible, so you may reach financial independence as soon as possible. Here, you want to maximize growth efficiency. Of course, this starts with finding those areas that work against your growth—draining your return potential. Most likely this is debt, such as credit card and student loan debt. After you attack those areas of your financial life, it's time to begin investing.

You may think it's time to run out and find a financial advisor to get you started. The reality is, most people don't need a financial advisor to help them establish retirement savings accounts and get invested. In this technology age, you can hop online and find a low-cost brokerage to open an IRA or Roth IRA; that is if your employer doesn't offer a retirement plan, and you start making systematic contributions (taking advantage of that dollar-cost averaging principle we talked about earlier). Statistically, most financial advisors, brokers and even the best money managers likely won't beat the index they use as their benchmark. They also usually won't beat the broader stock market as a whole. It may take a little reading, but if you are comfortable picking your own holdings or sticking with broader stock market index funds, you will keep costs low. In addition, it is probable you will beat most advisors out there to whom you would otherwise pay 1 or 2 percent per year.

If you're not comfortable building a portfolio yourself, there are plenty of robotic advisory firms that charge substantially less than the advisor down the street. They help pick the initial funds, rebalance regularly, and even conduct automatic tax harvesting, if necessary. Your primary goals are to keep your cost of investing low; that includes ongoing taxation, as well.

If you are in the minority of younger individuals with substantial incomes or are a business owner with tax planning concerns, then maybe it might be time to hire a financial advisor and justify the cost. The reality is, a financial advisor doesn't typically need to be hired until you require protection against major financial liabilities you are facing. When you are younger this is most likely death, disability, and taxation.

At Howard Bailey, we also have some younger clients who are 10-plus years out from retirement without a need for extensive financial planning.

MEET DAVE AND CHARLOTTE

For instance, I had a husband and wife who were 42 and 37, respectively, and visited my office for a second opinion regarding the direction they were headed for retirement. Dave and Charlotte did a wonderful job of saving and paying off debt over the years with substantial retirement accounts already built up. Dave handled most of the investing over the years using various low-cost mutual funds with a national online brokerage. They recently inherited some additional funds that increased the size of their investable assets by about fifty percent overnight. He invested the funds in the same way their other retirement accounts had been, but he felt anxious over the responsibility of being a "good steward" of their life savings. Moreover, Charlotte was uncomfortable with not having a back-up plan in case something happened to her husband. She did not understand finances and had no interest in picking up on the family investing if something happened to Dave.

I ran them through retirement projections—sharing with them what they would need to do to hit their retirement goals, along with some diversification recommendations. I will note, however, they were already doing perfectly fine. I shared with them that they did not need me to be successful at this stage of their lives. They weren't looking for more growth, but instead they wanted the sense of reassurance a partnership could provide. Everyone is different, and for this couple it made sense to get started with a financial advisor at a young age: one with whom they could sit down on a face-to-face basis and develop a lifelong relationship. Others may rather go it alone. But at some point, in your financial life, your goals will shift along with the risks that you face as you approach retirement. As you near retirement, you begin to shift your mindset and realize you will need to preserve the assets you worked a lifetime to accumulate transitioning from offense to defense.

Retirement Red Zone

When you get within five to ten years from retirement, you reach what is often referred to as "the Retirement Red Zone." You find yourself at a point in life where the mistakes made over the coming years could make or break your retirement. As retirement specialists, most families we work with are ready to begin structuring their retirement strategy or are already in retirement and prepared to implement a real plan for their future. The sooner you take the initiative to sit with an advisor and begin planning, the greater chance you will have to retire as planned. You may feel you have plenty of time to continue to take on the risks you have in the past, but the reality may be to the contrary.

MEET NATE AND ERICA

As an example, Nate and Erica visited with us five years out from retirement. They invested their entire retirement savings in their 401(k), and their investing position had been about the same for the last 20-plus years. We recommended they begin reallocating their 401(k) to reduce their overall risk level. Of course, a less aggressive investment position would likely reduce their long-term average rate of return. They had a substantial amount of their 401(k) funds invested into an employer stock fund. Nate felt the company was doing well and they always made up losses in past market crashes over a five-year period. We shared analysis with him illustrating that it wasn't just making up losses that would be necessary over the following five-year period. They would need to see a modest annual growth rate as well or they would not be able to retire as planned.

Nate and Erica followed our advice and reallocated their 401(k) with their first five years of income needs positioned in a fixed-income portfolio at minimal risk. Over the following 12 months, the employer stock lost nearly half its value due to organizational changes that were unforeseen by any of the employees. During their next review, Nate and Erica mentioned that many of their co-workers would not be able to retire as planned and would have to continue to work many more years. They, on the other hand, would be able to retire as planned due to their diversified allocations. Not only this, but over the coming years they never enjoyed their work as much as they did at that time. They no longer had the stress of worrying about whether retirement would work out or not and whether they were saving enough. Erica said it gave them great peace of mind knowing they could step away from work at any time as they were now in "Job Optional" status.

MEET TOM AND JENI

On another note, it pays to get a jump-start on your health care planning as well. This fact was illustrated to me directly after implementing a financial plan for a couple in their late 50s. When we first laid out Tom and Jeni's strategy, they heard their 60s were the best time to examine long-term health care solutions. At the meeting, they immediately questioned why we would implement a long-term care strategy before they reached that necessary age. Not even two months after putting their long-term health care strategy in force, Jeni was diagnosed with an aggressive form of cancer. While she would likely overcome the disease, she was unqualified for any life or long-term care insurance policy moving forward. Luckily, we already put their long-term care strategy in motion, so the diagnosis couldn't erase her chances at coverage.

Sometimes, retirement preparedness is more about organizing expenses and debt than anything else. When it comes to a successful retirement, you often hear it's all about a successful retirement income strategy. This is true, but that starts with identifying expenses. We visited with a couple who were several years from retirement, yet they didn't think they would ever retire due to their expenses in comparison to their savings. They had substantial credit card and mortgage debt that was sopping up large portions of their monthly budget. On a thorough review, we reorganized their debt, so they would pay it off by the time they wished to retire. We also freed up additional cash to put away for retirement. Now, they will retire on time with a new outlook on life and their golden years.

It's never too late to begin your retirement planning, and I would wrap estate planning into that strategy, as well. While I see many who are tempted to designate estate planning as a separate stage in their financial life, in my experience, this segmentation results in putting off decisions for scenarios that could occur much sooner than expected. We had a couple in their 80s who came to us assuming it was too late for them to do anything. They wanted to have a second look nonetheless. Together, they had roughly $3 million in various investment accounts, over $2 million of which was invested in taxable mutual funds. Their frustration was mostly with their annual tax bill. They were being taxed on mutual fund distributions they weren't spending in addition to substantial Required Minimum Distributions. I often state this as "spending money on money you're not spending." They were paying more taxes than they ever had throughout their lifetime. We managed to shelter those funds from ongoing taxation and structure a strategy to pass them on to their heirs tax-free, as well. In addition, they were able to take advantage of Qualified Charitable Distributions (QCDs) to satisfy charitable goals and eliminate their RMDs from their tax return. In the end, these relatively simple changes will most likely put tens, if not hundreds, of thousands of dollars back in their pockets over the remaining years of their lives— and all this after they thought nothing could be done. The moral of the story: While it's never too early to plan for a comprehensive and complementary retirement plan, it's never too late, either!

A Written Plan

Let me share with you a quick story. Maybe you've heard it before, but it's one of my favorites. Dr. Albert Einstein was traveling from New York to Chicago in the late 1920s—by train, of course. Einstein boarded the train and the conductor began passing through the cabin, collecting and punching tickets. As he approached Einstein, he noticed a concerned look on his face while shuffling through his pockets. The conductor recognized the famous doctor and told him not to worry about the ticket, as he knew he was good for it. While the conductor passed back through the cabin, he noticed Einstein still looking very disheveled, even more so than the last time he walked by. As Einstein stood on his chair looking through the luggage racks, the conductor said, "Dr. Einstein, please have a seat, we know who you are. Your ticket is really unnecessary." The concerned doctor replied, "Sir, I know who I am, the problem is I don't know where I am going!"

Based on the thousands of pre-retirees and retirees I

engage with each year, I estimate that fewer than 20 percent of retirees have a written plan for retirement. That written plan is your ticket for a successful retirement—your ticket to avoid the level of concern the conductor saw on Dr. Einstein's face. When you ultimately structure a retirement strategy, it should be put in writing, so you know not only what your destination is, but also how you will get there. A retirement plan is not a stack of statements. It's not a simulation stating you have a percentage chance of success, and it's certainly not an investment strategy. A retirement plan is documentation for how each of your assets will specifically assist you in retirement. Moreover, it lays out the main risks you will face during retirement and how you will overcome them as they occur. Where will you turn in case of emergency? Where will your income come from in case of a market downturn? Where will you generate additional income in case of inflation? How will you cover potential long-term care expenses? How will you manage ongoing taxation in addition to avoiding taxes as you leave those assets behind to the next generation?

Choosing the Right Financial Planner

I want to offer a few important points to keep in mind when you are trying to find the right financial advisor for you and your family. I'm not always the right fit for the people who come into our office, and they aren't always the right fit for us. This must be a mutual decision on behalf of both parties since you could be starting a lifelong relationship. That is, unless your advisor is nearing retirement age themselves—let's start there.

Age and Business Continuity

You may be surprised to learn that at the time I am writing this the average age of a financial advisor is fifty-one with 38 percent of advisors expecting to retire in the next ten years, according to a 2017 Forbes article referencing Cerulli Associates.[29] Currently, just 10 percent of financial advisors are under the age of thirty-five.

This means the majority of advisors will be retiring when they are supposed to be managing YOUR retirement. You don't want to be left looking for a new advisor when you're eighty-five years old.

Our team once saw a wave of new clients come to us from another advisory firm that was run by a gentleman who decided to up and retire one day. Most of these clients said their advisor was older than they were when they started working with him, yet they didn't think anything of it. One gal in particular, Shirley, explained that she didn't hire the advisor in the first place. Her husband did. She lost her husband a few years prior to the retirement of their advisor and she didn't know where to begin looking for a replacement. Shirley interviewed three other advisors before hiring our firm, and she said a key determinant for that was the average age of our team. This was in addition to knowing there was always someone prepared and ready, even if her primary advisor decided to retire. There is no question that experience is one of the most important aspects of finding the right advisor, but there should be no lack of emphasis placed on longevity as well.

Independence

It is incredibly important to find a financial advisor who is independent, not an employee of a large firm. There are many firms at which brokers and advisors can work. I started in the business as an employee of a large brokerage firm. Employees there were told what products and funds to recommend. We were told what we had to offer was perfect for everyone.

I soon came to realize this was the wrong approach, but unfortunately, this still occurs today. During those days, I often used a tool I was told to sell and would soon find that a tool my dad used as an independent financial advisor was less expensive and had more benefits!

Let's take, for example, a large Wall Street brokerage firm. First, if you work with such a firm, the people you work with are employees of that firm. Their primary responsibility is to that firm, not the client. Their job is to increase shareholder value for that firm.

You're just a customer. If you work with an independent financial advisor, then you are the only person to whom that advisor answers. An ethical independent advisor does not have an agenda or a list of stocks to push. It is vital that you work with an independent advisor who can always use the best tool for the job and answer only to you.

You may be apprehensive about working with an independent advisor. While you don't have the feeling of security that a big box name brand firm offers, you don't need to be concerned if you understand what to look out for. Every independent advisor should have what is known as a third-party custodian.

A third-party custodian can ensure that advisors don't take your money and run. A third-party custodian acts as an intermediary between the advisory firm and the client. Under this approach, your advisor will never handle client checks, deposits or withdrawals directly. In nearly every theft by an advisor from client funds, there was no third-party custodian involved.

In many instances, the client wrote checks made out in the financial advisor's name. To sum it up, a third-party custodian acts as the policeman—ensuring your funds stay in your name at all times. Some examples of the largest third-party custodians include Fidelity, Charles Schwab, Pershing, and TD Ameritrade. You can also be assured that you are always receiving a statement from these third parties and not directly from your advisor—where there is room for fabrication. In the end, the same degree of safety and security can be afforded for your life savings with an independent advisor, along with all the other benefits that come along with it.

Chemistry

Another prime consideration is "chemistry." It's very important that you feel the person you are talking to understands you. If you are a husband and wife, make sure the person talks to both of you. Make sure the advisor also listens to both of you. If for one moment you feel that a broker is dismissing you or your feelings, insulting you or coming across as arrogant, this is the wrong person to work with. You need to choose an advisor who understands you, listens to you and will put together a financial plan that fits your needs and goals. Remember, it's your money, not theirs!

Empathy

Does the advisor understand you and feel like you do when it comes to your important issues? You may have a special-needs child who requires special planning. You may come from a very poor family—one that lived through the Great Depression. You're worried about running out of money. Can that advisor relate? It's critical that the advisor listens and feels empathy for your particular fears. Another clue that you're working with the wrong advisor is if he or she does not understand or does not listen.

Community Recognition

The broker or advisor you choose should have a recognized name in the community. Let's think about a company like Google. In Palo Alto, if somebody even writes the word "Google" on a sign, Google comes after them to take that word down. Why? Google ensures it has the legal right to force the issue. For what reason? They will do it simply because they want to protect their reputation, which they feel is second to none. Other companies that have a very high level of brand recognition, such as McDonald's and Pepsi, will do almost anything to protect that brand.

Conscientious firms may decide not to take certain customers because they worry that those customers might be the complaining type. The companies want to protect both their reputation and brand. The same goes for financial advisors. Financial advisors who have a recognized name in a community will be very careful to bend over backward to do the right thing. Why? Because they spent years building their strong reputations, and they don't want anything to tarnish them. Choose an advisor who has a well-recognized name in the community.

Education

Not much is required to hang out one's shingle as a financial advisor. The unfortunate truth is many financial advisors lack the education, knowledge, credentials, and experience required to carry you through the ups and downs of your golden years. The bar for entry into the financial profession is set quite low. Many firms do not even require a college degree. Many states, in fact, require no formal education or certification at all to set up shop as a financial advisor. In contrast, however, some advisors put themselves through grueling, rigorous and extensive educational programs to obtain such designations as CERTIFIED FINANCIAL PLANNER™ professional and Chartered Financial Analyst (CFA®). So, asking for an advisor's education and experience is fundamental in your search. I believe it should be one of the first questions you ask.

In addition, there are literally hundreds of designations and certifications that are deceptively impressive. Many advisors hold impressive-sounding credentials, some of which represent impressive achievements, but most do not. Before selecting your advisor, make sure that you understand what his or her credentials really represent. For instance, a CERTIFIED FINANCIAL PLANNER™ professional must have:

- Graduated with a bachelor's degree (or higher) from an accredited college or university
- Successfully completed college or university-level coursework encompassing the areas of financial planning, insurance planning, investment planning, income tax planning, retirement planning, estate planning, interpersonal communication
- Completed the CFP® Board's Financial Plan Development Course, requiring presentation of a financial plan to the CFP® Board
- Completed a rigorous pass/fail exam administered at a secure facility

- Must have 6,000 hours of personal financial planning experience or 4,000 hours of apprenticeship experience that meets additional requirements
- Passed the CFP® Board's Fitness Standards for Candidates and Registrants
- Completed 30 hours of continuing education every two years

In sharp contrast, the Certified Retirement Financial Advisor Certification Board only requires a four-day classroom course—no prior work experience and no higher education. Although, you are required to complete 15 hours of continuing education per year, which can be taken online by simply bypassing the class and taking a quiz. While this designation may sound very similar to a CERTIFIED FINANCIAL PLANNER™, the two are in no way comparable. The financial services industry requires financial advisors to establish credibility with their clients. For this reason, an entire credentialing industry now exists to satisfy industry demand. Believe it or not, you could "earn" all these credentials in fewer than 30 days—no prior work experience required![30]

- CAC – Certified Annuity Consultant – one-day class
- APP – Asset Protection Planner – 12-hour online or in person
- LTCIS – Long-Term Care Insurance Strategist – two-day class
- AIF – Accredited Investment Fiduciary – two-and-one-half-day class
- CCPS – Certified College Planning Specialist – 18 to 25 hours self-study
- CWPP – Certified Wealth Preservation Planner – 24 hours online or in person
- CFG – Certified Financial Gerontologist – 24 hours self-study
- CSC – Certified Senior Consultant – 25 hours self-study

- CSA – Certified Senior Advisor – three-and-one-half-day "live" class

- AIFA – Accredited Investment Fiduciary Auditor – three-and-one-half-day class

- CDS – Certified Divorce Specialist – four-day workshop

- CRFA – Certified Retirement Financial Advisor – four-day class

Experience

The failure rate for legitimate financial advisors is incredibly high. It is one of the most difficult professions to succeed in—with the long hours and high level of education required. According to Andre Cappon, president of the CBM Group, only 15 percent of advisors in training make it through their fourth year. That is why I recommend you find an advisor with a minimum of five years in practice. Many financial advisors have a high level of sales experience and are extremely charismatic, but personality can only take you so far.

Compensation

We often think discussing payment is rude. After all, it's a big social faux pas to ask someone how much they get paid. Yet, when someone is performing a service for you—whether it's a doctor talking about surgery or a plumber talking about your bathroom remodel—you wouldn't think twice about asking questions like, "How much will this cost?" or, "Should we pay up front or wait for a bill?" The same should apply to your financial advisor; it shouldn't be a dark secret how much you pay for the service you receive.

There are three ways a financial advisor might get paid: fee only, commission based or fee based. Each has its own advantages and disadvantages, which I will briefly touch on. Your bottom line here is whether you trust your advisor and whether you believe you get an adequate level of service in return for what you pay.

Fee-only advisors charge clients directly through a consultation fee, an hourly rate, a charge for services or a payment based on the percentage of assets under their management. This helps advisors remain independent, but a tradeoff is that a fee-only advisor might be more aggressive in his or her approach because the more aggressively your portfolio grows, the more money goes in his or her pocket.

Commission-based advisors get a commission for sales, whether that is a percentage of assets assessed as an upfront fee, a kickback from a company whose product they sold or a surcharge for each stock purchase/sale a client makes. Sometimes, these advisors offer more diverse products, but the downside of this approach is that a commission-based advisor must always be selling, possibly incentivizing them to use products that have high turnover rates. There is also the potential for conflict of interests in offering a certain product that might have a higher commission than another.

Fee-based advisors do a little of both. They might charge a fee to write up a financial plan for a client and then receive a commission or fee when the client purchases those products. This gives the financial advisor incentive to grow a client's portfolio, but since his or her compensation isn't only based off assets under management, they have more leeway to seek conservative strategies. Of course, the potential conflict of interest regarding higher incentive commission products still exists.

There is no "perfect" compensation model, yet it is important to understand how your advisor makes money and how much will come from your pocket. You can then make a realistic determination about whether the service you receive is in line with what you pay.

For more information on advisor compensation models, check out some of the articles I wrote for the financial publication, Kiplinger, which are linked on the "Read" tab of the Howard Bailey website:

https://howardbailey.com/articles

Your Investment Team

When looking for your retirement advisor, recognize the value of a team approach. In retirement, your financial life becomes much more complicated. You will need to ensure that all your bases are covered—mainly those of taxation, estate planning and financial planning. Your retirement advisor should act as the quarterback of this team, assisting you with not only developing and implementing your plan, but bringing a team of experts to the table.

In the world of finance, we all have our areas of expertise. The Certified Public Accountant (CPA) has extensive experience in accounting and tax matters. The attorney who specializes in estate planning will naturally have extensive experience in estate law. Your financial professional should have general knowledge and experience in both, as well as in handling your investments. You will most likely need these experts to work as a team, with your financial advisor acting as quarterback or general contractor.

I will issue a note of caution, however. Be careful when you're exploring all-in-one firms. By this, I mean firms who boast having all the professionals you need under one roof. They might have a CPA, an estate planning attorney, a financial advisor, etc. all in one business. Even if the financial advisor in the office has a solid record, you will want to double-check the experience and credentials of each professional to find out how successful they are in their area of expertise. In my experience, the best CPAs and estate planners have their own firms. You'll want to be sure you're getting the "best in breed" of all these professionals. All too often, we find that these "comprehensive" offices may have one or two experienced principal professionals, but beware, check that the "tax professional" or "estate attorney" has some experience and isn't just someone's nephew who just passed the bar or received their certificate and needed a job.

Breaking Up With Your Accumulation Advisor

To borrow from the immortal lyrics of Neil Sedaka, "Breaking up is hard to do." If you are at or nearing retirement, and you have an accumulation advisor whose dialogue no longer makes good investing sense to you, it's time to break up. I know, changing financial advisors can be one of the most awkward and difficult situations you will experience since you broke up with your high school sweetheart. It's a little uncomfortable at first, spurned lover syndrome and all of that. They may beg, offering to do anything to meet your needs and win you back. A good line to use is that you "Still want to be friends," or "It's not you, it's me." It may be a difficult adjustment to make, sort of like a rock star changing barbers, but keep in mind, it's for the best. And once it's over, you can move on with your financial life and things will get better.

What's especially difficult is when you are going steady with your financial advisor all through your working years. But look at it this way—you no longer see a pediatrician when you reach adulthood, and you don't consult your podiatrist for dental work. We understand perfectly well when it's time to change doctors through the different stages of life, or when we experience an issue with our health. It's much the same when dealing with wealth issues. Just as doctors have their own areas of expertise, so do financial advisors. Whether they deal in risk or safety is something you must determine for yourself.

What if your advisor is your best friend? Well, I must admit—that is a tough one. It becomes a personal issue. You don't want to risk losing a good friend. On the other hand, you probably don't want to risk losing your money in retirement, either. So, it may come down to how much that friendship is worth in terms of dollars and cents. I do know some retirees who allowed their portfolio to continue to underperform for years because they didn't want to hurt anyone's feelings. But I've known others who concluded that if the friendship hinged on continuing a business relationship that was no longer mutually beneficial, then it was probably a shallow friendship to begin with. In the end, it's a personal decision.

"You just slip out the back, Jack
Make a new plan, Stan
You don't need to be coy, Roy
Just get yourself free
Hop on the bus, Gus
You don't need to discuss much
Just drop off the key, Lee
And get yourself free"

~Paul Simon, American singer/songwriter
"50 Ways to Leave Your Lover"[31]

The transition from one advisor to another can be made with a simple phone call, email or letter. Other times, you may want to introduce your previous advisor to your new advisor. This can be more pleasant than you might think because if your current advisor is truly a friend, he or she may recognize his or her limitations when it comes to handling your financial affairs. You may own a Lexus and have a special relationship with the folks who run the service department at the dealership. But, if you trade that Lexus in for a Mercedes, it is doubtful your pals at the old dealership will view you with contempt if you begin to take your automobile to the dealership that is fully certified and qualified to work on your car. Know when it is time to move on and recognize the importance of your financial future.

Summary

As you begin your journey down the path to financial security and independence, I want to leave you with this. I once met a successful business consultant who owned several businesses across the country—achieving wealth most of us can only dream of. He asked me what my number was. I had never been asked that question. I just tried to succeed and save the best way I thought I could. I realized I never really put a retirement plan together for myself to determine ultimately what number it was that I had to save to retire and not just retire but feel financially free.

He said, "Once you reach that number, you will be amazed by the success you will achieve." It was enlightening, really. We are trained to think that getting to that number IS success. He said, "When you get there, you will begin to treat your business, family, clients, friends and yourself differently." At some point, when it's no longer about the money, then you can change the world.

For me, I have been so unbelievably blessed—lucky some might say—that I am just getting there in my financial life. I'm beginning to see what he really meant, as it is changing all aspects of my life. Our business has begun to truly explode. We are able to give more back to our clients and provide services many financial firms simply won't because it's too expensive. We've lowered costs, undercutting other financial firms that are too driven by the bottom line. We also spend more time with our clients and prospective clients than other firms are willing to, as they are more worried about closing the next person walking through the door. We have the best staff we could ever imagine—providing better benefits and pay than our competitors, which in turn directly impacts the experience of the clients who choose to work with us.

In my personal life, I found ways to hire managers and staff to allow me to spend more time with my family than ever before. For years, I was in the office before the light came up and left after the sun went down seven days a week. When I first started working with my dad, I remember him picking me up at five in the morning and not getting home until midnight. Now, I get to take my kids out to the park during the week, get involved in church activities, and have relationship-building getaways that brought my wife and I closer than ever before—building the rock-solid marriage we've always wanted. It all started with a rock-solid Purpose-Based Retirement Plan allowing me to live the "Job Optional" lifestyle. The same can be true for you.

Regardless of your life stage, you can get there. I've seen people who were already there and didn't know they were. Once a real retirement plan illustrated that they MADE IT, it allowed them to live like they never thought they could. They spent more time with family, doing recreational activities they lost touch with, and even started second careers that fulfilled their dreams. The sooner you get started, the sooner you will get there.

Once you do, you will achieve levels of success in life you never thought possible. Here's to achieving financial independence and living your true PURPOSE, which I promise has nothing to do with money in the end.

CHAPTER 7: TAKEAWAYS, ACTIONS, AND NOTES

What are your biggest takeaways from this chapter?

_____

_____

_____

What are 3 action steps that you should work on now?

1. _____

2. _____

3. _____

What are 3 action steps for later?

1. _____

2. _____

3. _____

Notes:

_____

_____

_____

_____

_____

_____

ABOUT THE AUTHOR

Casey Weade is a sought-after retirement planning professional, speaker and CEO/Chief Visionary of the national financial firm, Howard Bailey. He hosts the "Retire with Purpose" radio, TV show and podcast—providing sound financial guidance to pre-retirees and retirees across the country. He is also a Certified Financial Planner™ (CFP®), Chartered Life Underwriter (CLU ®), Retirement Income Certified Professional® (RICP®), an Investment Advisor Representative, and holds licenses in Life, Accident, and Health insurance.

CASEY WEADE

Casey's not only passionate about guiding people toward a financially secure retirement, but he also zones in on what your Golden Years might look like. His "Purpose-Based Retirement" philosophy begins with finding your "why" and building a plan to protect that. In Casey's words, *"The path to retirement is all about utilizing offensive strategies. But once you actually get there, the game switches to defending your purpose for retirement and, in turn, your life savings from the major risks it will face."*

Casey is a lifelong Midwest native, and currently resides in Fort Wayne, IN, with his wife and two sons. He sponsors the Howard Bailey Junior Golf Tour as part of the Indiana Golf Foundation, and continues to stay active in his own community by supporting small businesses, local organizations and charities throughout the year.

More information on Casey, his various programs and speaking engagements can be found at RetireWithPurpose.com.

ACKNOWLEDGMENTS

Hundreds of hours have been poured into the content and development of what you just read. While I would like to take full credit for everything that has gone into this book, the reality is it would not have come to fruition without the support of hundreds of individuals in my life.

First, I would like to thank all the families and friends who have put their trust and faith into our organization as the quarterbacks of their financial lives. I hope they have learned as much from me as I have learned from them over the many years they have been working with our team. I have learned about marriage, friendship, business, and many more pieces of existential wisdom that I will pass on to as many people as I possibly can. My team and I could not have gotten where we are today without your support. And, to one of the first potential clients I ever met who told me I would not be a success in the business of financial planning until I was old and gray—thanks for giving me the motivation to persevere.

I could have never achieved an ounce of what I have to this day without the loving support of my wife, Chelsie. Since the day we met, she has patiently put up with the long hours I have put in growing the business we are so proud of, not to mention the time away I spent writing this book. Not only has she endured and encouraged the time I have devoted to our clients and business, but she herself has made this business a passion of her own. To share a passion with a spouse is a priceless commodity I will be forever grateful for.

Chelsie has blessed me with two beautiful boys, Calvin and Carver. These two have taught me more than I would ever have imagined. Calvin always lightens the mood, letting me reflect on the simpler things in life. Carver illustrates to me that, no matter how small we are, we can overcome any obstacle.

Obviously, none of this would be possible without the help of my parents bringing me into this world. My dad, Ron, has taught me the ropes and principles of finance starting at a very early age. He showed me how to be humble, curious, and driven to help others. My mom, Diann, imparted on me the importance of education and caring for others. She illustrated to me through her actions how to always be there to support others, just as she has for me my entire life.

I would be remiss to leave out the team at Howard Bailey Financial, Inc. Our advisory team has shown me there are many financial planners out there today who are ready and willing to put their heart and soul into the selfless relationships they build with others every day. Many thanks to our staff for putting up with my constant energy and demands as we continue to see massive growth that couldn't be managed without their help. My eternal appreciation is due to the entire team at Howard Bailey for their love and commitment to the families we work with and for embracing our philosophy of always doing the BEST thing.

WHO IS HOWARD BAILEY?

There truly is no Howard Bailey that we know of. The company name was created by Casey in honor of his two biggest childhood mentors. Together, their names represent the values and philosophy the company was founded upon.

Howard Weade is the grandfather of Casey Weade on his father's side. Howard lent much to the conservative investment approach that was ingrained in the mind of Casey, as well as the approach that the Howard Bailey team utilizes today.

Ralph **Bailey** is the grandfather of Casey Weade on his mother's side. Ralph's background in the local school system influenced the mentality that Howard Bailey upholds every day: focusing on educating clients and treating each as an individual.

The name also reflects Casey's family values. Casey founded Howard Bailey as a family company built upon developing a secure, independent retirement for each and every client.

HOWARD AND CHRISTINE WEADE

RALPH AND LORETTA BAILEY (W/CASEY WEADE)

A BACKGROUND ON ·HOWARD BAILEY

HOWARD BAILEY

RETIRE WITH PURPOSE

Founded by Casey Weade in 2011, Howard Bailey provides comprehensive financial planning strategies to pre-retired and retired individuals across the country. The Howard Bailey team focuses on helping individuals achieve total wealth optimization and reliable income sources in retirement, all the while zoning in on their "why". As a firm believer in establishing a clear purpose for an individual's financial future, Casey and his team offer a framework for identifying and most efficiently helping to defend against the biggest obstacles to one's financial freedom. They optimize current financial situations by looking for money that is falling through the cracks and create customized Purpose-Based Retirement plans to help provide individuals with the financial confidence to live in Job Optional* status.

For more information on how Casey and his team can help you achieve your Job Optional* retirement, visit www.howardbailey.com or call (866) 482-9559.

GLOSSARY

While I've done my best to avoid the jargon-loaded terminology of the financial industry, I've included some of the more worn out words and phrases that you might hear when conversing with any given financial services professional.

Note: Unless otherwise noted, all definitions are taken from the Investopedia.com dictionary web site.

Investopedia Dictionary, Investopedia, LLC., 2018,
119 West 40th Street
New York, NY 10018
https://www.investopedia.com/dictionary

401(k)

A 401(k) plan is a qualified employer-sponsored retirement plan that eligible employees may make salary-deferral contributions to on a post-tax and/or pretax basis. Employers offering a 401(k) plan may make matching or non-elective contributions to the plan on behalf of eligible employees and may also add a profit-sharing feature to the plan. Earnings in a 401(k) plan accrue on a tax-deferred basis.

529

A 529 plan provides tax advantages when saving and paying for higher education. There are two major types, prepaid tuition plans and savings plans. Prepaid tuition plans allow the plan holder to pay for the beneficiary's tuition and fees at designated institutions in advance. Savings plans are tax-advantaged investment vehicles, similar to IRAs.

Rules governing the plans are laid out in Section 529 of the Internal Revenue Code.

They are legally referred to as "Qualified Tuition Programs" and sometimes called "Section 529 plans."

accelerated death benefit provisions

An accelerated death benefit (ADB) is a benefit that can be attached to a life insurance policy that enables the policyholder to receive cash advances against the death benefit in the case of being diagnosed with a terminal illness. Many individuals who choose an accelerated death benefit have less than one year to live and use the money for treatments and other costs needed to stay alive.

annuity

An annuity is a financial product that pays out a fixed stream of payments to an individual, primarily used as an income stream for retirees. Annuities are created and sold by financial institutions, which accept and invest funds from individuals and then, upon annuitization, issue a stream of payments at a later point in time. The period of time when an annuity is being funded and before payouts begin is referred to as the accumulation phase. Once payments commence, the contract is in the annuitization phase.

Please Note: This is the commonly accepted definition, but flawed, as not all annuities result in annuitization or income streams.

assets

An asset is a resource with economic value that an individual, corporation or country owns or controls with the expectation that it will provide a future benefit. Assets are reported on a company's balance sheet and are bought or created to increase a firm's value or benefit the firm's operations. An asset can be thought of as something that, in the future, can generate cash flow, reduce expenses or improve sales, regardless of whether it's manufacturing equipment or a patent.

bonds

A bond is a fixed income instrument that represents a loan made by an investor to a borrower (typically corporate or governmental). A bond could be thought of as an I.O.U. between the lender and borrower that includes the details of the loan and its payments. A bond has an end date when the principal of the loan is due to be paid to the bond owner and usually includes the terms for variable or fixed interest payments that will be made by the borrower. Bonds are used by companies, municipalities, states, and sovereign governments to finance projects and operations. Owners of bonds are debtholders, or creditors, of the issuer.

cap rates

A cap is an interest rate limit on a variable rate credit product. It is the highest possible rate a borrower may have to pay and also the highest rate a creditor can earn. Interest rate cap terms will be outlined in a lending contract or investment prospectus.

cash flow

Cash flow is the net amount of cash and cash-equivalents being transferred into and out of a business. At the most fundamental level, a company's ability to create value for shareholders is determined by its ability to generate positive cash flows, or more specifically, maximize long-term free cash flow.

certificates of deposit

A certificate of deposit (CD) is a savings certificate with a fixed maturity date, specified fixed interest rate and can be issued in any denomination aside from minimum investment requirements. A CD restricts access to the funds until the maturity date of the investment. CDs are generally issued by commercial banks and are insured by the FDIC up to $250,000 per individual.

certified financial planner

A certified financial planner (CFP) refers to the certification owned and awarded by the Certified Financial Planner Board of Standards, Inc. The CFP designation is awarded to individuals who successfully complete the CFP Board's initial and ongoing certification requirements. Individuals desiring to become a CFP professional must take extensive exams in the areas of financial planning, taxes, insurance, estate planning, and retirement.

conservative fixed income properties

Fixed income is a type of investment whose return is usually fixed or predictable and is paid at a regular frequency like annually, semi-annually, quarterly or monthly. Along with equities, fixed income forms an important part of the investment market and is used for raising capital by the companies and governments. Compared to the uncertain returns from equities, commodities and other investment classes, the predictable and regular returns from fixed-income investments can be used to efficiently diversify one's portfolio.

cost-push inflation

Aggregate supply is the total volume of goods and services produced by an economy at a given price level. When there is a decrease in the aggregate supply of goods and services stemming from an increase in the cost of production, we have cost-push inflation. Cost-push inflation means prices have been "pushed up" by increases in costs of any of the four factors of production (labor, capital, land or entrepreneurship) when companies are already running at full production capacity. With higher production costs and productivity maximized, companies cannot maintain profit margins by producing the same amounts of goods and services. As a result, the increased costs are passed on to consumers, causing a rise in the general price level (inflation).

CPA

Certified Public Accountant (CPA) is a designation given by the American Institute of Certified Public Accountants to those who meet education and experience requirements and pass an exam.

For the most part, the accounting industry is self-regulated. The CPA designation helps enforce professional standards in the industry. Other countries have certifications equivalent to the certified public accountant. For example, in Canada, the equivalent to a CPA is Chartered Accountants (CA)

default

Default is the failure to pay interest or principal on a loan or security when due. Default occurs when a debtor is unable to meet the legal obligation of debt repayment, and it also refers to cases in which one party fails to perform on a futures contract as required by an exchange.

defined contribution plans

A defined-contribution plan is retirement plan that's typically tax-deferred, like a 401(k) or a 403(b), in which employees contribute a fixed amount or a percentage of their paychecks in an account that is intended to fund their retirements. The sponsor company will generally match a portion of employee contributions as an added benefit to help retain and attract top talent. These plans place restrictions that control when and how each employee can withdraw from these accounts without penalties.

demand-pull inflation

Demand-pull inflation occurs when there is an increase in aggregate demand, categorized by the four sections of the macroeconomy: households, businesses, governments and foreign buyers. When these four sectors concurrently want to purchase more output than the economy can produce, they compete to purchase limited amounts of goods and services. Buyers, in essence, "bid prices up" again, causing inflation. This excessive demand, also referred to as "too much money chasing too few goods," usually occurs in an expanding economy.

dividends

Ordinary dividends are a share of a company's profits passed on to the shareholders on a periodic basis. Ordinary dividends are taxed as ordinary income and are reported on Line 9a of the Schedule B of the Form 1040. All dividends are considered ordinary unless they are specifically classified as qualified dividends.

down market

A stock market which is falling or is at its lowest level.

"down market" *InvestorWords.com*. WebFinance, Inc. November 07, 2018 <http://www.investorwords.com/9500/down_market.html>.

equity

- A stock or any other security representing an ownership interest. This may be in a private company, in which case it is a private equity.

- On a company's balance sheet, the amount of the funds contributed by the owners or shareholders plus the retained earnings (or losses). One may also call this stockholders' equity or shareholders' equity.

- In margin trading, the value of securities in a margin account minus what the account holder borrowed from the brokerage.

- In real estate, the difference between the property's current fair market value and the amount the owner still owes on the mortgage. It is the amount that the owner would receive after selling a property and paying any liens. Also referred to as "real property value."

- In investment strategies, equities are one of the principal asset classes. The other two classes are fixed-income (bonds) and cash/cash-equivalents. These are used in asset allocation planning to structure a desired risk and return profile for an investor's portfolio.

- When a business goes bankrupt and has to liquidate, equity is the amount of money remaining after the business repays its creditors. This is most often called "ownership equity," but some call it risk capital or "liable capital."

ERISA

The Employee Retirement Income Security Act of 1974 protects Americans' retirement assets by implementing rules that qualified plans must follow to ensure plan fiduciaries do not misuse plan assets. Under ERISA, plans must provide participants with information about plan features and funding, and regularly furnish information free of charge.

FCU

A federal credit union (FCU) is a credit union regulated and supervised by the National Credit Union Association (NCUA). The NCUA is a federal government agency with authority designated by the Federal Credit Union Act of 1934 to oversee the national credit union system in the United States. The NCUA provides chartering for U.S. credit unions similar to the chartering process by the Office of the Comptroller of the Currency for national banks.

FDIC

An FDIC Insured Account is a bank or thrift (savings and loan association) account that meets the requirements to be covered by the Federal Deposit Insurance Corporation (FDIC). The type of accounts that can be FDIC-insured include negotiable orders of withdrawal (NOW), checking, savings and money market deposit accounts; and certificates of deposit (CDs). The maximum amount that is insured in a qualified account is $250,000 per depositor, per FDIC-insured bank and per ownership category. That means if you have up to that amount in a bank account and the bank fails, the FDIC makes you whole from any losses you suffered. Any sum that exceeds $250,000 should be spread among multiple FDIC-insured banks.

fixed annuity

A fixed annuity is a type of annuity contract that allows for the accumulation of capital on a tax-deferred basis. In exchange for a lump sum of capital, a life insurance company credits the annuity account with a guaranteed fixed interest rate while guaranteeing the principal investment. A fixed annuity can be annuitized to provide the annuitant with a guaranteed income payout for a specified term or for life.

flexible withdrawal strategy

Systematic withdrawal allows a shareholder to withdraw money from an existing mutual fund portfolio. With a systematic withdrawal plan, a fixed or variable amount is withdrawn at regular intervals. Withdrawals can be made on a monthly, quarterly, semiannual or annual schedule. Often, a systematic withdrawal plan is used to fund living expenses during retirement. The holder of the plan may choose withdrawal intervals based on his or her commitments and needs.

FRA

Forward rate agreements (FRA) are an over-the-counter contract between parties that determines the rate of interest, or the currency exchange rate, to be paid or received on an obligation beginning at a future start date. The FRA determines the rates to be used along with the termination date and notional value. FRAs are cash settled with the payment based on the net difference between the interest rate and the reference rate in the contract. The notional amount is not exchanged.

FRB

The Federal Reserve Board is the governing body of the Federal Reserve System.

The FRB is considered an independent agency of the federal government. The Fed has a statutory mandate to maximum employment and stable prices at moderate long-term interest rates, and the FRB chair and other officials frequently testify before Congress, but it makes monetary policy independently of the legislative or executive branches and is structured like a private corporation.

guaranteed lifetime withdrawal benefit

A Guaranteed Lifetime Withdrawal Benefit (GLWB) is a rider to an annuity contract that allows for lifetime guaranteed withdrawals to be made from an annuity during the owner's lifetime without penalty. The owner typically pays for the GLWB with an extra percentage of fees of the total value of the annuity contract.

hedge funds

A hedge fund is basically a fancy name for an investment partnership. It's the marriage of a professional fund manager, who can often be known as the general partner, and the investors, sometimes known as the limited partners, who pool their money together into the fund.

immediate annuity

An immediate annuity, also called an income annuity or single premium immediate annuity (SPIA), is a type of annuity designed to provide guaranteed income payments that must begin between one month and one year after purchase. The purchase of an immediate annuity is usually an irrevocable decision that cannot be undone once the free-look period has expired following contract issue.

"Immediate Annuities "*AnnuityAdvantage*,1999-2018,

https://www.annuityadvantage.com/annuity-type/immediate-annuities/?gclid=Cj0KCQiA2o_fBRC8ARIsAIOyQ-mdcRhsvSEhwWEIxgRWoIQVxbyifa0JR0bUQ_IDKuubVTmeSpFLUp4aAsLnEALw_wcB.

index funds

An index fund is a type of mutual fund with a portfolio constructed to match or track the components of a market index, such as the Standard & Poor's 500 Index (S&P 500). An index mutual fund is said to provide broad market exposure, low operating expenses and low portfolio turnover. These funds adhere to specific rules or standards (e.g. efficient tax management or reducing tracking errors) that stay in place no matter the state of the markets.

inflation

Inflation is the increase in the prices of goods and services over time. It's an economics term that means you have to spend more to fill your gas tank, buy a gallon of milk, or get a haircut. Inflation increases your cost of living.

Amadeo, Kimberly. "Inflation, How It's Measured and Managed", *The Balance*, the Dotdash publishing family, November 07, 2018, https://www.thebalance.com/what-is-inflation-how-it-s-measured-and-managed-3306170.

inflation hedge

An inflation hedge is an investment that is considered to provide protection against the decreased purchasing power of a currency that results from the loss of its value due to rising prices (inflation). It typically involves investing in an asset that is expected to maintain or increase its value over a specified period of time. Alternatively, the hedge could involve taking a higher position in assets, which may decrease in value less rapidly than the value of the currency.

interest

Interest is the charge for the privilege of borrowing money, typically expressed as annual percentage rate (APR). Interest can also refer to the amount of ownership a stockholder has in a company, usually expressed as a percentage.

IRA

An individual retirement account is an investing tool individual use to earmark funds for retirement savings. There are several types of IRAs as of 2018: traditional IRAs, Roth IRAs, SIMPLE IRAs and SEP IRAs. Sometimes referred to as individual retirement arrangements, IRAs can consist of a range of financial products such as stocks, bonds or mutual funds. A self-directed IRA is a type of traditional or Roth IRA that allows investors to make all of the investment decisions for their account and affords access to a broader range of investments, such as real estate, private placements and tax liens.

junk bonds

A junk bond is a fixed-income instrument that refers to a high-yield or noninvestment-grade bond. Junk bonds carry a credit rating of BB or lower by Standard & Poor's (S&P), or Ba or below by Moody's Investors Service. Junk bonds are so called because of their higher default risk in relation to investment-grade bonds.

large cap stock

Large cap (sometimes "big cap") refers to a company with a market capitalization value of more than $10 billion. Large cap is a shortened version of the term "large market capitalization." Market capitalization is calculated by multiplying the number of a company's shares outstanding by its stock price per share. A company's stock is generally classified as large cap, mid cap or small cap.

life insurance

Life insurance is a contract between an insurer and a policyholder in which the insurer guarantees payment of a death benefit to named beneficiaries upon the death of the insured. The insurance company promises a death benefit in consideration of the payment of premium by the insured.

liquidation

Liquidation in finance and economics is the process of bringing a business to an end and distributing its assets to claimants. It is an event that usually occurs when a company is insolvent, meaning it cannot pay its obligations when they come due. As company operations end, the remaining assets are used to pay creditors and shareholders, based on the priority of their claims.

living will

A living will—also known as an advance directive—is a legal document that specifies the type of medical care that an individual does or does not want in the event he or she is unable to communicate his or her wishes.

longevity risk

1. The risk that a pension fund or life insurance company takes on by offering its plans, due to the chance that the company could end up paying out more than anticipated due to increasing life expectancy. The risk is particularly high for any plans that ensure lifetime benefits for the recipient.

2. The risk that the amount of money an individual saves for retirement might not be enough to sustain them, due to increased life expectancy.

"longevity risk" *InvestorWords.com*. WebFinance, Inc. November 08, 2018 <http://www.investorwords.com/6856/longevity_risk.html>.

long-term bonds

A debt security with a maturity in the long-term. While there is no set definition of what constitutes the long-term, it is generally accepted that long-term bonds are those that mature several years in the future, often more than 15 or 20. One of the most low-risk long-term bonds, the U.S. Treasury Bond, usually has a maturity of 30 years.

"Long-Term Bond." *Farlex Financial Dictionary*. 2009. Farlex 8 Nov. 2018 https://financial-dictionary.thefreedictionary.com/Long-Term+Bond

managed account

A managed account is an investment account that is owned by an individual investor and overseen by a hired professional money manager. In contrast to mutual funds, which are professionally managed on behalf of many mutual-fund holders, managed accounts are personalized investment portfolios tailored to the specific needs of the account holder. With a mutual fund, the fund company hires a money manager who looks after investments in the fund's portfolio and may alter the fund's holdings in accordance with its objectives.

MEC

A modified endowment contract (MEC) is a tax qualification of a life insurance policy whose cumulative premiums exceed federal tax law limits. The taxation structure and IRS policy classification changes after becoming a modified endowment policy.

Morningstar

Morningstar is a Chicago-based investment research firm that compiles and analyzes fund, stock and general market data. They also provide an extensive line of internet, software, and print-based products for individual investors, financial advisors and institutional clients. The research reaches all corners of the world, including North America, Europe, Australia, and Asia. Among its many offerings, Morningstar's comprehensive, one-page mutual and exchange-traded fund (ETF) reports are widely used by investors to determine the investment quality of the more than 2,000 funds.

mortality and expense charge

A mortality and expense risk charge is a variable annuity fee included in certain annuity or insurance products that compensates the insurance company for mortality risks and other various risks and expenses it assumes under the annuity contract.

mutual funds

A mutual fund is an investment vehicle that is made up of a pool of funds collected from many investors for the purpose of investing in securities such as stocks, bonds, money market instruments and similar assets. Mutual funds are operated by money managers who invest the fund's capital and attempt to produce capital gains and income for the fund's investors.

NCUA

National Credit Union Administration or the NCUA is an agency of the United States federal government. The federal government created the NCUA to monitor federal credit unions across the country.

NOLHGA

National Organization of Life and Health Insurance Guaranty Associations (NOLHGA) is a voluntary organization of U.S. life and health insurance guaranty associations. Founded in 1983, it covers policyholders when a multistate life or health insurance company fails.

non-deductible IRA

A nondeductible IRA is in many ways the same as a traditional IRA. The contribution limits are the same, the money grows tax-deferred, which means you don't pay taxes on gains or dividends and to be eligible to contribute, you must have received earned income.

The difference is, with a nondeductible IRA, you aren't allowed to deduct your contribution from your income taxes like you can with a traditional IRA. However, you'll avoid capital gains and dividend taxes as your money grows. The downside of a nondeductible IRA is, the money that you would've saved on those tax deductions could've been compounding over the years.

"What Is A Nondeductible IRA?", *Retirement Living Information Center*, 1998 – 2018, RetirementLiving.com, LLC https://www. retirementliving.com/what-is-a-nondeductible-ira.

non-qualified annuity

An annuity or pension plan that one buys individually rather than through an employer. Nonqualified plans are not subject to the same restrictions as qualified plans. As a result, withdrawal penalties are smaller or non-existent, and one may continue to make contributions to a more advanced age (sometime until the annuitant is over 80). In the United States, specific restrictions on nonqualified plans are set at the state level. The IRS does not regulate them; as a result, contributions are not tax-deductible, but earnings still are.

"Nonqualified Annuity." *Farlex Financial Dictionary*. 2009. Farlex 8 Nov. 2018 https://financial-dictionary.thefreedictionary.com/ Nonqualified+annuity

oil and gas partnerships

Oil and gas partnerships are some of the most lucrative partnerships in the world. If one enters into the right partnership, the chances of earning a good profit as a result of the partnership are quite high. Statistics estimate that the world demand for oil and gas increased substantially in the last decade and continues to do so every year. Moreover, the current oil fields are yielding less oil; too little to completely satisfy the whole oil demand. As such, entering a successful oil partnership is something worth an investor's time.

"Oil Partnerships" *Oil Well Investment Companies* 2013, http://www.oilwellinvestmentcompanies.com/oil-partnerships.shtml

overfunded cash value life insurance policy

An overfunded life insurance policy is a Whole or Universal Life insurance policy (or variation of those, such as Indexed Universal Life) in which more premium is paid in than required to secure the death benefit. An overfunded policy will generate cash value faster and can possibly increase the death benefit or dividends. People often use overfunded life insurance for tax favored income during retirement. There is the chance that you can overfund it too much and turn your policy into a Modified Endowment Contract (MEC), which takes away the favorable tax treatment of life insurance. If you are going to overfund your policy, work with an experienced life insurance agent who can help you set up the policy to your maximum benefit.

Mace Peggy "What Is an Overfunded Life Insurance Policy?" *InsuranceLibrary*, InsuranceLibrary.com LLC, October 7, 2013, http://www.insurancelibrary.com/life-insurance/what-is-an-overfunded-life-insurance-policy

pension

A pension is a fund into which a sum of money is added during an employee's employment years, and from which payments are drawn to support the person's retirement from work in the form of periodic payments. A pension may be a "defined benefit plan" where a fixed sum is paid regularly to a person, or a "defined contribution plan" under which a fixed sum is invested and then becomes available at retirement age.

"Wikipedia" Pension, *Wikimedia Foundation, Inc.*, 30 July 2018, https://en.wikipedia.org/wiki/Pension

probate

A probate is a legal process in which a will is reviewed to determine whether it is valid and authentic. Probate also refers to the general administering of a deceased person's will or the estate of a deceased person without a will. The court appoints either an executor named in the will (or an administrator if there is no will) to administer the process of collecting the assets of the deceased person, paying any liabilities remaining on the person's estate, and finally distributing the assets of the estate to beneficiaries named in the will or determined as such by the executor.

proprietary produce

A power of attorney (POA) is a legal document giving one person (the agent or attorney-in-fact) the power to act for another person (the principal). The agent can have broad legal authority or limited authority to make legal decisions about the principal's property, finances or medical care. The power of attorney is frequently used in the event of a principal's illness or disability, or when the principal can't be present to sign necessary legal documents for financial transactions.

A person appointed as power of attorney is not necessarily an attorney. The person could just be a trusted family member, friend or acquaintance.

qualified charitable distributions (QCD)

A qualified charitable organization is a nonprofit organization that qualifies for tax-exempt status according to the U.S. Treasury. Qualified charitable organizations include those operated exclusively for religious, charitable, scientific, literary or educational purposes, or for the prevention of cruelty to animals or children, or the development of amateur sports.

Nonprofit veterans' organizations, fraternal lodge groups, cemetery and burial companies and certain legal corporations can also qualify. Even federal, state and local governments can be considered qualified charitable organizations if the money donated to them is earmarked for charitable causes.

rate of return

A rate of return (ROR) is the net gain or loss on an investment over a specified time period, expressed as a percentage of the investment's initial cost. Gains on investments are defined as income received plus any capital gains realized on the sale of the investment.

The formula for rate of return is:

$$\text{Rate of Return} = \frac{\text{Ending value of investment} - \text{Beginning value of investment}}{\text{Beginning value of investment}} \times 100$$

This simple rate of return is sometimes called the return on investment, or ROI. Taking into account the effect of the time value of money and inflation, the real rate of return can also be defined as the net amount of discounted cash flows received on an investment after adjusting for inflation.

real-estate investment trusts

Real estate investment trusts ("REITs") allow individuals to invest in large-scale, income-producing real estate. A REIT is a company that owns and typically operates income-producing real estate or related assets. These may include office buildings, shopping malls, apartments, hotels, resorts, self-storage facilities, warehouses, and mortgages or loans. Unlike other real estate companies, a REIT does not develop real estate properties to resell them. Instead, a REIT buys and develops properties primarily to operate them as part of its own investment portfolio.

"Real Estate Investment Trusts (REITs)." *Investor.gov*, www.investor.gov/introduction-investing/basics/investment-products/real-estate-investment-trusts-reits.

reinsurance

Reinsurance, also known as insurance for insurers or stop-loss insurance, is the practice of insurers transferring portions of risk portfolios to other parties by some form of agreement to reduce the likelihood of paying a large obligation resulting from an insurance claim. The party that diversifies its insurance portfolio is known as the ceding party. The party that accepts a portion of the potential obligation in exchange for a share of the insurance premium is known as the reinsurer.

revenue sharing agreement

Revenue sharing takes many different forms, although each iteration involves sharing operating profits or losses among associated financial actors. Sometimes, revenue sharing is used as an incentive program—a small business owner may pay partners or associates a percentage-based reward for referring new customers, for example. Other times, revenue sharing is used to distribute profits that result from a business alliance. Revenue sharing is also used in reference to Employee Retirement Income Security Act (ERISA) budget accounts between 401(k) providers and mutual funds.

revocable living trust

Revocable living trusts serve two important functions in estate planning. The first is to provide for the potential disability of the grantor. The second is to avoid probate of the grantor's estate at death. As a practical matter, for many individuals, planning for incapacitation may be significantly more important than avoiding probate.

When you create a revocable living trust, you are the trustee of the trust until you die or become incapacitated. Upon either of those events, a successor trustee will take over without the necessity for a guardianship or probate. If no plans are made for potential incapacitation, control of a person's assets is taken out of their hands and placed in the authority of a guardian and supervising court.

RMD – Required Minimum Distribution

A required minimum distribution is the amount that traditional, SEP or SIMPLE IRA owners and qualified plan participants must begin withdrawing from their retirement accounts by April 1 following the year they reach age 70 1/2. The retiree must then withdraw the RMD amount each subsequent year based on the current RMD calculation.

ROTH IRA

Named for Delaware Senator William Roth and established by the Taxpayer Relief Act of 1997, a Roth IRA is an individual retirement plan (a type of qualified retirement plan) that bears many similarities to the traditional IRA. The biggest distinction between the two is how they're taxed.

Traditional IRA contributions are generally made with pretax dollars. You usually get a tax deduction on your contribution and pay income tax when you withdraw the money from the account during retirement. Conversely, Roth IRAs are funded with after-tax dollars; the contributions are not tax deductible—although you may be able to take a tax credit of 10 to 50% of the contribution, depending on your income and life situation. But when you start withdrawing funds, qualified distributions (see below) are tax free.

S&P 500

The S&P 500 Index (formerly Standard & Poor's 500 Index) is a market-capitalization-weighted index of the 500 largest U.S. publicly traded companies by market value. The index is widely regarded as the best single gauge of large-cap U.S. equities. Other common U.S. stock market benchmarks include the Dow Jones Industrial Average or Dow 30 and the Russell 2000 Index, which represents the small-cap index.

security

A security is a fungible, negotiable financial instrument that holds some type of monetary value. It represents an ownership position in a publicly-traded corporation (via stock), a creditor relationship with a governmental body or a corporation (represented by owning that entity's bond), or rights to ownership as represented by an option.

separated/unified managed account

An SMA is a portfolio of assets managed by a professional investment firm. In the United States, the vast majority of such firms are called registered investment advisors and operate under the regulatory auspices of the *Investment Advisors Act* of 1940 and the purview of the U.S. Securities and Exchange Commission (SEC). One or more portfolio managers are responsible for day-to-day investment decisions, supported by a team of analysts, operations and administrative staff.

A unified managed account (UMA) is a professionally managed

private investment account that can include multiple types of investments all in a single account. Investments may include mutual funds, stocks, bonds and exchange traded funds. Unified managed accounts are often rebalanced on a specified schedule.

single premium immediate annuity

An immediate annuity, also known as an income or single premium immediate annuity (SPIA), is a contract between you and an insurance company designed for income purposes only. Unlike a deferred annuity, an immediate annuity skips the accumulation stage and begins paying out income either immediately or within a year after you have purchased it with a single, lump-sum payment. SPIAs are also called immediate payment annuities, income annuities, lifetime annuities, and immediate annuities.

Silvestrini, Elaine. "What is a Single Premium Immediate Annuity?" *Single Premium Immediate Annuities*, Annuity.org, September 28, 2018, https://www.annuity.org/annuities/immediate/.

spreads (hurdles)

A hurdle rate is the minimum rate of return on a project or investment required by a manager or investor. The hurdle rate denotes appropriate compensation for the level of risk present; riskier projects generally have higher hurdle rates than those that are less risky.

In hedge funds, the hurdle rate refers to the rate of return that the fund manager must beat before collecting incentive fees.

stocks

A stock is a share in the ownership of a company. Stock represents a claim on the company's assets and earnings. As you acquire more stock, your ownership stake in the company becomes greater.

stretch IRA

A stretch IRA is an estate planning strategy that extends the tax-deferred status of an inherited IRA when it is passed to a non-spouse beneficiary. It allows for continued tax-deferred growth of an Individual Retirement Account (IRA). By using this strategy, an IRA can be passed on from generation to generation while beneficiaries enjoy tax-deferred and/or tax-free growth. The term "stretch" does not represent a specific type of IRA; rather it is a financial strategy that allows people to stretch out the life—and therefore the tax advantages—of an IRA.

surrender charge period

The surrender period is the amount of time an investor must wait until he or she can withdraw funds in excess of the free withdrawal amount from an annuity without facing a penalty. Surrender periods can be many years long and withdrawing money before the end of the surrender period can result in a surrender charge, which is essentially a deferred sales fee. Generally, but not always, the longer the surrender period, the better the annuity's other terms.

treasury bonds

A treasury bond (T-bond) is a marketable, fixed-interest U.S. government debt security with a maturity of more than 10 years. Treasury bonds make interest payments semiannually, and the income received is only taxed at the federal level. Treasury bonds are known in the market as primarily risk-free; they are issued by the U.S. government with very little risk of default.

treasury inflation protected securities

Treasury inflation protected securities (TIPS) refer to a treasury security that is indexed to inflation in order to protect investors from the negative effects of inflation. TIPS are considered an extremely low-risk investment because they are backed by the U.S. government and because the par value rises with inflation, as measured by the Consumer Price Index, while the interest rate remains fixed.

trust

A trust is a fiduciary relationship in which one party, known as a trustor, gives another party, the trustee, the right to hold title to property or assets for the benefit of a third party, the beneficiary. Trusts are established to provide legal protection for the trustor's assets, to make sure those assets are distributed according to the wishes of the trustor, and to save time, reduce paperwork and, in some cases, avoid or reduce inheritance or estate taxes. In finance, a trust can also be a type of closed-end fund built as a public limited company.

undistributed tax liability

The term "undistributed PFIC earnings tax liability" means, in the case of any taxpayer, the excess of—

(A) the tax imposed by this chapter for the taxable year, over

(B) the tax which would be imposed by this chapter for such year without regard to the inclusion in gross income under section 1293 of the undistributed earnings of a qualified electing fund.

"SEC. 1294. ELECTION TO EXTEND TIME FOR PAYMENT OF TAX ON UNDISTRIBUTED EARNINGS" Expat Tax Tools Form 8621 Calculator. Expat Tax Tools, Inc, 2018, https://www.form8621.com/codes-and-regulations/pfic-us-code-1294-election-to-extend-time-for-payment-of-tax-on-undistributed-earnings/.

unified managed account

A unified managed account (UMA) is a professionally managed private investment account that can include multiple types of investments all in a single account. Investments may include mutual funds, stocks, bonds and exchange traded funds. Unified managed accounts are often rebalanced on a specified schedule.

variable annuity

A variable annuity is a type of annuity contract that allows for the accumulation of capital on a tax-deferred basis. As opposed to a fixed annuity that offers a guaranteed interest rate and a minimum payment at annuitization, variable annuities offer investors the opportunity to generate higher rates of returns by investing in equity and bond subaccounts. If a variable annuity is annuitized for income, the income payments can vary based on the performance of the subaccounts.

END NOTES

1 *Mutual Funds are sold by prospectus. Please consider the investment objectives, risks, charges, and expenses carefully before investing in Mutual Funds. The prospectus, which contains this and other information about the investment company, can be obtained directly from the Fund Company or your financial professional. Be sure to read the prospectus carefully before deciding whether to invest.*

2 Asset Allocation does not guarantee a profit or protect against a loss in a declining market. It is a method used to help manage investment risk.

3 Fixed Annuities are long term insurance contacts and there is a surrender charge imposed generally during the first 5 to 7 years that you own the annuity contract. Withdrawals prior to age 59-1/2 may result in a 10% IRS tax penalty, in addition to any ordinary income tax. Any guarantees of the annuity are backed by the financial strength of the underlying insurance company.

4 Dollar cost averaging may help reduce per share cost through continuous investment in securities regardless of fluctuating prices and does not guarantee profitability nor can it protect from loss in a declining market. The investor should consider his/her ability to continue investing through periods of low price levels.

5 *Exchange Traded Funds (ETF's) are sold by prospectus. Please consider the investment objectives, risks, charges, and expenses carefully before investing. The prospectus, which contains this and other information about the investment company, can be obtained from the Fund Company or your financial professional. Be sure to read the prospectus carefully before deciding whether to invest.*

6 Guarantees provided are based on the claims-paying ability of the issuing company.

7 Board of Governors of the Federal Reserve System. Nov. 3, 2017. "Reserve Requirements." https://www.federalreserve.gov/monetarypolicy/reservereq.htm.

8 Practicing Law Institute. "Insurance Regulation in a Nutshell." https://www.pli.edu/emktg/toolbox Insur_Reg22.doc.

9 NOLHGA. Nov. 15, 2011. "Insurance Oversight Legislative Proposals: Testimony for the Record of The National Organization of Life and Health Guaranty Associations Before the House Financial Services Subcommittee on Insurance, Housing and Community Opportunity."

10 Peter G. Gallanis. NOLHGA. June 5, 2009. "NOLHGA, the Life and Health Insurance Guaranty System, and the Financial Crisis of 2008-2009." https://www.nolhga.com/resource/code/file.cfm?ID=2645.

11 https://hbr.org/2014/07/the-crisis-in-retirement-planning

12 Indexed annuities are insurance contracts that, depending on the contract, may offer a guaranteed annual interest rate and some participation growth, if any, of a stock market index. Such contracts have substantial variation in terms, costs of guarantees and features and may cap participation or returns in significant ways. Any guarantees offered are backed by the financial strength of the insurance company. Surrender charges apply if not held to the end of the term. Withdrawals are taxed as ordinary income and, if taken prior to 59 ½, a 10% federal tax penalty. Investors are cautioned to carefully review an indexed annuity for its features, costs, risks, and how the variables are calculated.

13 Indices are unmanaged and investors cannot invest directly in an index. Unless otherwise noted, performance of indices do not account for any fees, commissions or other expenses that would be incurred. Returns do not include reinvested dividends.
The Standard & Poor's 500 (S&P 500) is an unmanaged group of securities considered to be representative of the stock market in general. It is a market value weighted index with each stock's weight in the index proportionate to its market value.

14 This chart is a hypothetical representation of fixed index annuity growth of $100K under varying market/index conditions and is not meant to represent the performance of any specific product. The black line shows the S&P® 500 annual return rate from 2000-2017, according to data from Yahoo Finance (https://yhoo.it/2SJ61Bm). The grey line shows the annual point-to-point strategy with 50% market participation. Participation rates are usually found in point-to-point indexing strategies. The higher the participation rate, the more interest you will be credited with when the market index (S&P® 500 for example) is moving up. Let's say that you were offered an uncapped, point-to-point account with a 50% participation rate. If the chosen index increased by 10%, then you would receive 50% of the gain or a 5% rate of return on your money that year. If the S&P® had a negative return, than zero interest would be credited to the fixed index annuity.

15 Riders are available for an additional fee - some riders may not be available in all States.

16 ***Please consider the investment objectives, risks, charges, and expenses carefully before investing in Variable Annuities. The prospectus, which contains this and other information about the variable annuity contract and the underlying investment options, can be obtained from the insurance company or your financial professional. Be sure to read the prospectus carefully before deciding whether to invest.***

The investment return and principal value of the variable annuity investment options are not guaranteed. Variable annuity sub-accounts fluctuate with changes in market conditions. The principal may be worth more or less than the original amount invested when the annuity is surrendered.

17 https://retirewithpurpose.com/podcast/wade-pfau-reverse-mortgages/

18 Roger G. Ibbotson. Zebra Capital Management. January 2018. "Fixed Indexed Annuities: Consider the Alternative." Summary on WealthManagement.com: http://www.wealthmanagement.com/insurance/ibbotson-fixed-indexed-annuities-beat-out-bonds

19 Not associated with or endorsed by the Social Security Administration or any other government agency.

20 https://hbr.org/2014/07/the-crisis-in-retirement-planning

21 Michael Kitces. Nerd's Eye View. Nov. 2, 2016. "Using Age Banding to Estimate How Spending Will Decline in Retirement." https://www.kitces.com/blog/age-banding-by-basu-to-model-retirement-spending-needs-by-category/

22 Tim McMahon. InflationData.com. June 16, 2016. "Gold and Inflation." https://inflationdata.com/ Inflation/Inflation_Rate/Gold_Inflation.asp

23 "Everything you need to know about 401(k) fees", MarketWatch, Inc, Apr 7, 2018, https://www. marketwatch.com/story/everything-you-need-to-know-about-401k-fees-2018-03-30

24 "Everything you need to know about 401(k) fees", MarketWatch, Inc, Apr 7, 2018, https://www. marketwatch.com/story/everything-you-need-to-know-about-401k-fees-2018-03-30

25 Bernicke, Ty A., "The Real Cost Of Owning A Mutual Fund", Bernicke, Ty A., Forbes Media LLC, Apr 4, 2011, https://www.forbes.com/sites/gradsoflife/2018/11/01/futureproofing-why-this-company-sources-talent-locally-and-why-you-should-too/#13803cf74cb2

26 https://www.forbes.com/2011/04/04/real-cost-mutual-fund-taxes-fees-retirement-bernicke. html#7f2b1e183244

27 Family Caregiver Alliance. National Center on Caregiving. "Selected Long-Term Care Statistics." https://www.caregiver.org/selected-long-term-care-statistics.

28 Genworth Financial. 2017. "2017 Cost of Care Survey." https://www.genworth.com/about-us/ industry-expertise/cost-of-care.html

29 https://www.forbes.com/sites/halahtouryalai/2017/07/25/amcricas-next-gen-wealth-advisors-millennials-who-survived-2008-are-now-managing-billions/#6a5940272d1a

30 For more information, read my article in Kiplinger's: https://www.kiplinger.com/article/investing/ T023-C032-S014-don-t-be-fooled-by-impressive-financial-credential.html

31 https://www.azlyrics.com/lyrics/paulsimon/50waystoleaveyourlover.html
Paul Simon lyrics are proper and copyright of their owners.
"50 Ways to Leave your Lover" lyrics provided for educational purposes and personal use only.

190

NOTES

194

NOTES

NOTES